WINNING BLACKJACK FOR THE SERIOUS PLAYER

To Harvey Adelman

ABOUT THE AUTHOR

Edwin Silberstang is acknowledged by the top professionals in the gambling world as a leading authority on games in America. His first book, *Playboy's Book of Games*, published in 1972, was an instant best seller and a selection of the Book of the Month Club. Since then, Silberstang has published over forty books dealing with games, gambling and the Vegas scene including *Winning Poker for the Serious Player*, also for Cardoza Publishing. His expertise has been used in the entertainment world, and he was the technical adviser on the film, *Big Town*, a story about a young gambler starring Matt Dillon, produced by Columbia Pictures.

In addition, he has written and starred in his own videos about gambling, and has appeared on many television and radio shows throughout the country. He is constantly called upon as a consultant and teacher as well.

Silberstang's success in the field of gambling writing comes from a skill as a novelist combined with a vast knowledge of gambling. His writing is clear and concise and he not only is able to present information but to make it interesting and fascinating. Now he brings his expertise to blackjack, where he is considered one of the great players and writers on the game.

WINNING BLACKJACK FOR THE SERIOUS PLAYER

EDWIN SILBERSTANG

CARDOZA PUBLISHING

Cardoza Publishing is the foremost gaming and gambling publisher in the world with a library of more than 200 up-to-date and easy-to-read books and strategies. These authoritative works are written by the top experts in their fields and with more than 10,000,000 books in print, represent the best-selling and most popular gaming books anywhere.

2011 NEW EDITION!
Copyright ©1993, 2000, 2002, 2011 by Edwin Silberstang
- All Rights Reserved -

Library of Congress Catalog Number: 2011925858
ISBN 10:   1-58042-284-5
ISBN 13: 978-1-58042-284-0

Visit our website or write for a full list of Cardoza Publishing books and advanced strategies.

CARDOZA PUBLISHING
P.O. Box 98115, Las Vegas, NV 89193
Toll-Free Phone (800)577-WINS
email: cardozabooks@aol.com
www.cardozabooks.com

TABLE OF CONTENTS

INTRODUCTION

Blackjack stands apart from all other games the casino offers, for it is the only one, which, when played against the house, involves a great deal of skill. In fact, the skill factor is so great that if a player uses correct strategy, he or she can beat the casino.

All the other games, such as roulette, craps and baccarat are games of pure luck and all are so structured that the house has an edge over the player which it never relinquishes. And all the other games have no memory—that is, what happened prior to the present spin of the wheel, play of the cards or roll of the dice, doesn't influence what will happen next.

However, blackjack is a game where the player may have an edge over the casino, and may take advantage of that edge by raising his bets. In that way, he can win more money when he is favored to win. When the casino has an edge in certain situations, the same player can reduce his wager, at his option, and thus minimize his losses.

Why, you may ask, if the house knows the game can be beaten, do they allow it to be played? A good question.

Even though blackjack can be beaten, few players take the time to study it properly, and fewer still know how to really play the game. Therefore, the casino still makes a ton of money off poor and unskilled players.

In this book, we're going to show you everything you'll need to know to beat the game. We'll show you a correct Basic Strategy for all blackjack games you might encounter, whether you play in Las Vegas, Northern Nevada, Atlantic City, on the riverboats, in Indian casinos, or any other jurisdiction that has legalized blackjack.

In addition to correct basic strategy, we'll introduce you to a simple but powerful counting method which will instantly inform you whether or not the cards are in your favor or favorable to the house. Then we'll show you how to alter your bets to take advantage of this.

Finally, we'll show you how to disguise your skill so that the casino allows you to play and take away their money.

Everything is in this book, from correct strategy to ways to tip the dealer, from betting methods to getting comped by the casino, that is, getting free meals, shows and even rooms. By the time you finish this book, you're going to be a winner at one of the best and most exciting games the casino offers.

Read on and be a winner!

THE BASICS OF BLACKJACK

THE DECK OR DECKS OF CARDS

Blackjack, or **21**, as it is often called, is played with an ordinary deck of 52 cards in which the jokers have been removed. There are four suits; spades, hearts, diamonds and clubs, but the suits have no intrinsic value. An ace of spades has the same value as an ace of hearts.

There are thirteen cards in each suit—the ace, 2, 3, 4, 5, 6, 7, 8, 9, 10, jack, queen and king.

In some casinos only one deck is used. In the majority of casinos, multiple decks of four or more are dealt. But even if multiple decks are used, the composition of the decks remain the same.

THE VALUE OF THE CARDS

Cards have individual values, according to their spots or numbers, with a few exceptions. The 2, 3, 4, 5, 6, 7, 8 and 9 each has its individual value. A 9 is worth 9 and 6 worth 6, for purposes of counting the value of a hand. A

10, jack, queen and king each has a value of 10, and from now on we'll refer to any of these cards as a **10** or **10-value card**.

Since there are four cards of each rank except for the 10, jack, queen and king, which make up sixteen 10-value cards, the 10s dominate the game, and special regard must be given to them in any strategy used for beating the casino.

Last, but most important, we've saved the ace for discussion. It alone among all the cards has a dual value. It can count as 1 or as 11, at the option of the player. Having this dual value makes it the most important and powerful of all cards in blackjack. It also has another powerful function. Combined with any 10-value card, the hand becomes a blackjack, the strongest of all hands. But we'll get into this later.

The important thing to know for now is that each card from the 2 to the 9 has its individual value, the 10, jack, queen and king all have 10-values, and the ace may be valued as a 1 or 11, at the player's option.

THE ORIGINAL HAND

So far, we've discussed individual card values. But in blackjack, the original hand dealt to the player or by the dealer to himself consists of two cards. The total of these two cards must be added together in order to determine future strategy. In the game of casino blackjack, if a player is not satisfied with his two-card total, he may **draw** or **hit** the hand to improve it.

We mentioned before that the game is also called 21. That is the highest total allowed for any valid hand. If a player's total value goes over 21, he is said to have a **bust hand**, or to have **busted**.

However, a player cannot bust with just the two cards dealt to him originally. The highest total he can have is 21, or a **blackjack**, if he is dealt a 10 and an ace. This is an immediate winner and the most desirable of all hands.

The next highest original total is 20, which consists of either two 10s or an ace and a 9, with the ace counting as 11.

HARD TOTALS AND HANDS

A **hard hand** is any hand in which there are no aces or where the ace is valued as a 1. Here are several examples of hard hands.

• 10-5	Hard 15
• 10-5-3	Hard 18
• 9-8	Hard 17
• 10-3-2-Ace	Hard 16
• 8-5-2-Ace-Ace	Hard 17

In the last two hands the ace counted as a 1, because to count it as an 11 would give a total over 21 and bust the hand. The other hands had no aces and were simple hard hands.

When a player plays his hand he doesn't have to announce that he has a hard total, or that he is using his ace as a 1 rather than an 11. It will be obvious to him and to the dealer, who won't question him as to how he wants to value his ace.

For example, a player is dealt 9-5 and hits and gets a

2 for a 16 total. He hits again and gets an ace. He now has a 17. Even if he mistakenly believes he has busted and shows his hand to the dealer, the dealer will tell him he has only a 17 and not a bust hand.

It is wise to practice adding up the totals of the hands, especially with an ace or aces involved, to get a better feel of the game.

SOFT TOTALS AND HANDS

A **soft hand** is any hand in which the ace is counted as an 11, or, if more than one ace has been dealt to that hand, at least one of the aces is counted as an 11.

Let's give this example: The player is dealt Ace-6. He now has a soft 17, with the ace counting as an 11. If he hits this hand and gets another ace, thus holding Ace-6-Ace, he now has a soft 18, because one of the aces (it really doesn't matter which) is valued as an 11.

Most of the time, however, the player will only be dealt one ace in a hand. Thus, a hand such as an Ace-5-2 is a soft 18, with the ace counting as an 11, plus the other 7 valued points. With at least one ace in any original two-card holding, the player, if he wishes, can draw another card without worrying about busting, for he cannot go over 21.

For example, a player is dealt the following hand: Ace-7 for a soft 18. If he hits this hand, and gets a 6, the ace now reverts to a 1 and his total is 14. Remember, the player can use his ace as a 1 or 11 to best suit his hand and make the most of his cards.

A soft hand can turn into a hard hand. We saw this in the previous example, where a soft 18 turned into a hard

14. It is a hard hand because now the ace is valued as a 1.

Most of the problems you'll encounter are valuing your soft totals. But with a little practice and experience it's easy to figure out the total value of your hand.

BUSTING

Busting is going over 21 and losing. A player can only have a valid hand if it is 21 or less. The same holds true for the dealer.

By the rules of blackjack, if a player busts, he loses immediately. If a dealer busts, he loses only to those players who have remained with valid hands. Thus, if you bust and subsequently in the same round of play the dealer busts, it doesn't help you. You have lost.

The question then is—why draw or hit your hand if you're in danger of busting? For example, anytime you have a hard total of 12 or more, you're in danger of busting if you hit. For example, if you have 9-3, and hit, any 10 you draw will bust your hand. So why do it?

As we shall see, there is a basic strategy at play in blackjack, and there are times when you must take the chance of busting in an endeavor to improve your total points.

> *If both you and the dealer bust in the same round of play the dealer busts, it doesn't help you. You have lost.*

THE BLACKJACK

An original hand of two cards, either held by the player or the dealer, which consists of an ace and a 10-value card is a **blackjack**. It is also known as a **natural**, or in slang terms, as a **snapper**. This is the strongest hand in the game.

If a player holds a blackjack, he is paid off at 3-2 for the hand. If he had $20 out as his bet, he will receive $30. If he had $25 bet, he'll get $37.50. He'll always get the exact 3-2 payout even if it involves being paid off in 25¢ pieces.

Every other bet in blackjack is paid off at even money. If the dealer has a blackjack and the player doesn't, the dealer wins the hand but doesn't get any enhanced payoff. He simply collects the player's losing bet. Therefore, with the 3-2 payout, getting a blackjack is one of the player's key goals.

When a player discovers he has a blackjack, in a game where the cards are dealt face down, he should immediately turn over his cards and claim his payout. If the cards are dealt face up, the dealer will see the blackjack and pay off the player correctly.

If the player and the dealer both have a blackjack at the same time, neither wins from the other. It's called a **push**, a tie, a standoff.

There are times when a player will get a hand of Ace-10 that is not a blackjack. This occurs when it is not the original hand dealt to the player. For example, the player has several options that we'll discuss later on. These include splitting pairs. If a player splits a pair of aces and gets a 10 on an ace, all he has in this instance is a 21, not

a natural. A blackjack can only be claimed on the original hand dealt.

THE OBJECT OF THE GAME

To put it as simply as possible, the object of blackjack is to win. To win you have to beat the dealer, who represents the casino and its bankroll.

In order to beat the dealer, one of two events must occur. First of all, your total must be higher than the dealer's. For example, you hold a 10-10 for a 20 and the dealer holds a 9-8 for a 17. You win. Your total is higher than the dealer's.

The second way to win is to have a valid hand, any valid hand, while the dealer busts. For example, suppose you hold an 8-4 and the dealer busts, or goes over 21. You win.

The reason you can hold relatively weak totals and still beat the dealer is that the dealer is bound by strict rules of play, from which he cannot deviate. We shall study these rules later on, for they help us form our basic winning strategy.

To put it as simply as possible, the object of blackjack is to win. To win you have to beat the dealer.

What happens if both you and the dealer have the same total? Suppose you hold 10-9 and the dealer holds Ace-8. Both of you have 19s. It's a tie, known as a **push**. Neither of you win. It's strictly a standoff. You don't get the dealer's money and more importantly, he doesn't get yours.

3

THE CASINO GAME

INTRODUCTION

This book is geared to casino blackjack, not the private game, which has different rules of play. In casino black-jack it's you, the player, against the dealer. The dealer rep-resents the house. You beat the dealer, you beat the house. Simple premise. You beat the house, you win money. Equally simple.

THE BLACKJACK TABLE

The game is played on a table about six feet long and sort of oval in shape. The following is what a blackjack table looks like.

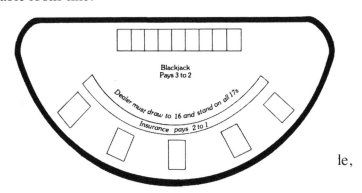

le,

though some casinos have their own color schemes. Green is the best, however, for it is the most soothing of colors to the human eye, and looking at cards for any length of time is hard on the eyes, let alone having to operate in the glare of a harsh red, for instance.

At the top of the table, we see a series of rectangles, which stand for the **rack**. This is where the casino chips are stored, and used by the dealer to pay the players' winning bets, or, having collected losing bets, storing them.

The dealer stands behind the rack, facing the players.

Not shown are several items which you will see when you play blackjack in a casino. As you look at the rack, to its right will be a slot, where cash is deposited into a **drop box**. A player may come to the game with cash and have the dealer exchange it for **casino chips**, also called **casino checks**.

Or a player may play with cash, and if it is lost, it will end up in the drop box rather than in the rack. If a player bets with cash, and wins, he will be paid off with chips, for two reasons. First of all, it's easier to figure out. If a player puts down several bills, they have to be carefully separated and counted by the dealer, as well as turned over to make sure they're genuine.

Secondly, chips are abstract symbols, while the cool green cash we know can buy the essentials of life. It doesn't seem as bad to lose chips as to depart with cash. Playing with chips makes gamblers into bigger players.

If a game is played with four or more decks, instead of a deck or two decks held in the dealer's hand, the cards will be dealt from a **shoe**. This is a plastic device which allows the dealer to easily deal out one card at a time in

> *When you are dealt a 10 together with an ace, a blackjack, you will get $3 for every $2 bet.*

a smooth manner. The shoe is always to the dealer's left, and thus to the right of the rack as we look at it on the page.

In most casinos, the cards already played, the **discards**, will be placed in a plastic case, on the other side of the dealer, to his right. This is a pretty standard feature at a casino blackjack table.

Below the rack, we see the notation, *Blackjack pays 3 to 2*. This means that when the player is dealt an original holding of a 10 together with an ace, a blackjack, he will get $3 for every $2 he has bet.

Next we see the notation *Dealer Must Draw to 16 and Stand on All 17s*. This means that if the dealer holds any hand below 17 he must automatically hit it till his total is 17 or better. Then he must stand. Let's explain this with a couple of examples.

Suppose the dealer holds a 10-2. He has a total of 12, and by the rules of the game, must hit the hand. Let's say he draws another card and that card is a 4. He now holds 10-2-4 for a 16. He must still hit, because his total is below 16. Suppose he hits and gets a 9. He is over 21 — he has busted.

Let's assume that the dealer holds the following hand: A-3. He has a soft 14, so he must hit. He hits and gets an ace. Now he holds A-3-A or a soft 15. He hits again and gets a 2. Now he holds an A-3-A-2 or a soft 17. He must use one of the aces as an 11. He can't value his hand as a 7, using both aces as 1s. Since he has a 17, by the rules of this casino he must stand.

In some casinos the dealer must also hit all soft 17s. This will be spelled out on the felt cover as follows: *Dealer must draw to all 16s and soft 17s*. If that is the case, in the previous example of A-3-A-2, with a soft 17, the dealer must hit again. As we shall see, when a dealer must hit soft 17s, it is a slight disadvantage to the player. The next notation we see says *Insurance Pays 2 to 1*.

We'll skip this for the time being and cover it later in our section on Insurance Bets.

Finally we see rectangular boxes at the edge of the table.

In our illustration, we see five of them. Each box represents a place or **spot** for a player. The table illustrated holds five players; other tables may hold up to seven players. In front of each box (not shown) is a chair or stool for the player to sit on while playing.

The players sit and the dealer stands during play, though a player may want to stand also. Some nervous types do stand; I remember seeing a hyperactive individual who not only stood but paced around talking to himself while playing. Blackjack draws all kinds.

Before we go into the actual game, let's discuss the dealer and his duties.

4

THE DEALER'S DUTIES

INTRODUCTION

The **dealer** represents the house and its bankroll. The dealer is thus an agent of the casino; he or she is on the casino's side and not the player's, but because dealers accept tips, their loyalties may waver.

At one time dealers were men, but now you're just as likely to face a woman as a man. In Northern Nevada it seems the majority of blackjack dealers are women. Of course it makes no difference to a player what sex the dealer is. What the player wants is an honest game by a dealer who isn't obtrusive, cold or insulting. In other words, it pays to face a human being rather than a robot.

CHANGING CASH FOR CHIPS

When a player comes to the table, he or she usually has cash in hand. Some players will be coming from other games or tables with casino chips, but most likely, with cash. The cash is put down on the table, not handed to the dealer and it is placed so that it isn't in a player's box.

If you put it in the player's box, a dealer may think you're making a bet and deal you cards. A competent dealer should always ask a new player bringing cash to a table if he wants chips for the cash.

To avoid any misunderstanding, place the money away from the box, and say, "Give me change." Say it loud enough for others to hear so that if the dealer missed your statement and dealt you cards, you have witnesses. I knew someone who came to the table, said these words and placed down $1,000 in $100 bills. He was dealt cards, which happened to be a blackjack. He had a no-lose situation. He collected $1,500 at 3-2. If he had a miserable hand, he would have protested that he wanted change. But don't take this chance. Say "give me change" loud and clear.

The dealer will take your cash and count it, turn it over to make sure it's real, and not a $20 on front and a $1 bill on the back (it happens). He or she will tell you the amount that has been counted, so you can verify it also, and then give you the equivalent in casino chips. The cash will then be placed on the slot to the dealer's left and dropped into the drop box.

The dealer, before giving you chips, may ask you what denomination you desire. For example, if you're at a $5 minimum game, and give the dealer $200, you might ask for nickels and quarters. This will show you're not a greenhorn. **Nickels** mean $5 chips and **quarters** $25 chips.

A competent dealer should always ask a new player bringing cash to a table if he wants chips for the cash.

The first duty of the dealer is to give chips for cash when the player comes to the table. However, his most important duty is running the game.

RUNNING THE GAME

Before a round of cards is dealt, the dealer will shuffle up the cards thoroughly and then present them to any of the players to be cut, Let's assume there are five players at the table. It is immaterial which one cuts the cards. Some players, through superstition, always refuse to cut the cards.

After the cards are cut by one of the players, the dealer restacks them, then, before dealing, burns the top card. By **burn** we mean he takes the top card and puts it out of play, either by placing it under the deck face up, or more usually, sliding it into the discard box to his right.

Burning a top card is customary, and prevents either the dealer or player from knowing its value and acting upon it.

In multiple deck games, the cut is made by a player inserting a colored card, not one that can be played, into the decks at any point he desires. The dealer then squares the cards and inserts them into the shoe. When that colored shuffle card is reached, the dealer knows that the cards are to be reshuffled.

Then the dealer makes sure that each of the players has made a bet in the box in front of him or her.

SINGLE DECK PLAY

Satisfied that the bets have been made, the dealer deals out one card face down to each player in turn, starting with the player to his far left, known as the **first baseman**, and proceeding in turn to the player at his far right, known as the **third baseman** or **anchorman**.

After each player has received one card in this manner, he deals himself a card also face down, then repeats the process, giving a second card to the first baseman and a second card to each subsequent player, and finally, giving himself a second card, face up.

This second dealer card, seen by all the players, is known as the **upcard**, and its value is important in the determination of what strategy should be used in playing out the player's hand. But for now, we'll concentrate on the dealer's duties.

After each player has received two cards face down, the first one to act is the first baseman, the first player to get cards.

If this player is satisfied with his total, he slides the cards under his chips as an indication that he wants no more cards. If he wanted to hit his hand, he'd scratch the two cards towards himself on the felt surface, and would then receive another card.

These two things, sliding cards under the chips or sliding cards on the surface, are standard, for in a noisy casino, words may be misinterpreted, but these moves are not.

If a player hits his hand and goes over 21 by busting, he should immediately turn over his cards and have them removed by the dealer. If a player is dealt a blackjack, an ace and 10-value card, he should also turn over his cards to collect $3 for every $2 he has bet.

MULTIPLE DECK PLAY

> *In multiple deck blackjack games the cards are generally dealt face up to the players.*

We have previously shown how the single deck game is played. In practically all single deck games the cards are dealt face down. However, in multiple deck games, which pretty much are the standard in most casinos in most jurisdictions, there are different moves which the player must make.

First of all, the cards are generally dealt face up to the players, therefore, players who desire another card point their index finger at the cards. The dealer will give them another card automatically. After a player is satisfied with his or her total, he simply waves his hand palm down over his cards.

If a player goes over 21 he has to do nothing, since the dealer sees the total. Likewise, if the player is dealt a blackjack, he is paid off at 3-2 without having to make any move.

THE DEALER'S ACTIONS

After all the players have played out their hands, whether in single or multiple deck games, the dealer then turns his attention to his own two cards. He turns over the face-down card, known as his **hole card**, for all the players to see. Let's assume he showed a 7 as his upcard and turned over a 9 as his hole card, for a 9-7 total of 16. By the rules of the game he must hit this total. Let's say he hits and gets a 2 for a total of 18. He must now stand.

Now, starting with the first baseman, he turns over

each player's cards to see their totals. In some casinos, he may first turn over the third baseman's cards. This is immaterial, but the dealer will always deal first to the first baseman, who will always act first on his hand. Of course in multiple deck games, the dealer need not turn over the players' cards since he sees their totals.

Let's assume that the first baseman has busted, so the second seated player's cards are turned over. He has a 19 and is paid off at even-money. The next player holds a 16 and loses his bet. His chips go into the rack. The fourth player holds 10-10 and wins his bet at even-money. The last player holds 10-8 and thus ties the dealer. It's a push, and there is a standoff, with no one winning.

After making payoffs and collecting losing bets, the dealer now deals another round of cards. After a few rounds, when the cards are nearly depleted in a single deck game, the dealer gathers the discards with the remaining cards in his hand and reshuffles the deck. Then the same procedure is followed, with the cards being cut, restocked, the players making bets and the cards being dealt out again. In a multiple deck game with so many more cards to be dealt, the dealer shuffles much more infrequently.

In all casinos, if the dealer's upcard is other than a 10-value card or an ace, he won't peek at the hole card, but will immediately be involved with the players' actions on their hands. For example, if the upcard is an 8, the dealer will look to the first baseman for his play.

However, should the dealer hold a 10-value card as his upcard, in many single deck and multiple deck casinos, he'll peek at the hole card before allowing the players to make their plays. This is done to see if he has a blackjack,

an immediate winner for the dealer, which will negate the player's moves.

It used to be a universal move on the part of the dealer to peek at his hole card if he had a 10 showing, but more and more casinos make him play out the game with the players before turning over his hole card.

In some casinos he only has an upcard and gets the hole card after all the players have acted on their hands. This rule is in force to prevent collusion between the dealer and players, so that the players don't find out what the hole card is, an enormous advantage for them.

Or even if there isn't collusion, sharp players can get information about the dealer's hole card from the way he peeks at it, or the way he might replace the cards after he has peeked. To give an example. If the dealer has a 10 as his upcard and sees a king of spades underneath as his hole card, he only has to see the border of that king to know he doesn't have an ace for a blackjack, so this move can be accomplished rather quickly.

But should he have a 4 of diamonds in the hole, the dealer might have to take a long look, since the 4 most resembles the ace. A discerning player can spot the difference in time devoted to peeking and act on his hand accordingly.

When a dealer holds an ace as his upcard, in most casinos he must immediately peek at the hole card after asking the

> *It used to be a universal move on the part of the dealer to peek at his hole card if he had a 10 showing, but more casinos make him play out the game with the players before turning over his hole card.*

players if they want insurance. This option will be dealt with fully under Player's Options later. If the dealer has a blackjack, then play stops and the dealer either collects losing bets or declares a push if any player also holds a blackjack.

However, in games where the hole card is not examined by the dealer, the players act on their hands without knowing of the dealer has a blackjack. If the dealer subsequently finds he has a blackjack, he collects from all players who do not also have a blackjack. For those players who took insurance, the bet is a push.

OTHER CASINO PERSONNEL

The dealer wears the house uniform, but there are other casino personnel who supervise the games and are of higher rank in the casino organization.

The next up in rank is the **floorman**. He is dresses in civilian clothes, usually a suit, shirt and tie, or a sports jacket, shirt and tie. The floorman supervises a group of tables within the **blackjack pit**, which is the total section of the casino devoted to blackjack in any one area of the casino.

The floorman has several duties. He can extend credit to a player, or verify the player's credit. He can **comp** the player, that is, offer him or her free services of the casino, such as a free meal, and even a free room if the player bets enough money.

If there is a dispute between a player and a dealer, the floorman has the authority to settle it. He also watches the games to make certain that no cheating is going on. He watches also to see that no card counters or extremely

skillful players are beating the house. A **card counter** is a player who keeps track of certain cards so that he knows if the deck is favorable or unfavorable to the player. We shall deal with card counting in a separate section, for it is an important component of winning.

The floorman can take countermeasures against a skillful player or even **bar** him; that is, stop him from playing in the casino. Again, countermeasures and barring will be covered in a separate section that shows the reader how to avoid having these moves applied to him.

Above the floorman in rank is the **pit boss**. He is in charge of the entire blackjack pit, and his authority is final in any dispute. He may also approve or verify credit for a **high roller**, a big gambler. The casinos call these players **premium players**. The biggest of all premium players are known as **whales**. A whale would be someone betting thousands of dollars on each card he plays.

Another person the player will come in contact with is the cocktail waitress. She is there to provide drinks of any kind to players while they are gambling. The drinks are free, and tipping is the usual way to reward these women.

BETS, BETTING LIMITS AND PAYOFFS

As we have noted, bets are usually made with casino chips, though cash may be used. However, all payoffs on winning bets are made with casino chips. If a cash bet is made and lost, the money is removed from the table and dropped through a slot into a drop box.

All games are not alike in any casino as far as betting limits are concerned. There are tables set aside for certain minimum bets.

The smallest minimum bet allowed in certain casinos is $1. Some casinos will not permit $1 bets and require a minimum of $2. Other casinos, such as those on the Las Vegas Strip, may have only $5 tables as their minimum tables.

> *There are tables reserved for players who may want to play one or all of the spots with at least a thousand dollars a spot.*

In addition to these tables, there may be $25 or $100 minimum tables set aside for bigger bettors. This doesn't necessarily mean better players, just bigger bettors. Generally speaking, the smaller table minimums attract beginners and players who aren't sophisticated. Bigger bettors and more skillful players don't like to associate with beginners who make mistakes and slow down the game.

There are even some tables reserved for an individual player who may want to play one or all of the spots at that table with at least a thousand dollars a spot.

When you go to a casino table, make sure that the table minimum is comfortable for you. If you have $200 to play with, you don't want to be at a $25 or $100 table where a few quick losses will deprive you of your entire bankroll. On the other hand, with $200, a $5 table is preferable to a $2 table, for the players will be a bit more sophisticated and the game will move along faster.

There are standard chips used by most casinos. They range from $1 to $500 chips. Generally speaking, the smallest are $1 and $5, known as **silver** and **nick-els**, or **redbirds**. $25 chips are known as quarters or **greenies**. $100 chips are known as **dollars**. Note that each denomination is downgraded as to value, with a $5 chip known as a nickel and $25 chips known as a quarter. The casino does this to disparage the amount a player bets.

When you're in a casino, there will always be bigger players than yourself. There'll be players betting thousands of dollars on each hand. Don't be intimidated by them. You play your game and play it at a comfortable level. It's better to be a $500 winner than a $100, 000 loser.

When you're at a particular minimum table, there generally will be a maximum limit bet stated on a small placard on the blackjack table. There is usually a lot of room between a minimum and maximum bet. A placard might read: $5-$1,000.

That gives you plenty of leeway. At a $25 table, you might see: $25-$3,000.

Sometimes, when you're at a table, the minimum limits will be changed. I was playing at a casino in downtown Las Vegas, at a $25 minimum table, **head-to-head** with the dealer, that is, alone against the dealer, when a Chinese woman who knew me vaguely, smiled and sat down to play.

She was an extremely wealthy woman, and immediately the placard was changed to $500 minimum. But I was allowed to play, since I had been sitting there, and I could play at my lower minimum. It didn't hurt that she liked me and insisted that I stay to bring her good luck.

She was an interesting case. She played only with cash, which she took out of a paper bag by the handful and laid out on several spots on the table. If the dealer got a blackjack, she tore up her cards and new cards had to be put in the game. But no matter how crazy she acted, it was true that I was lucky for her. And she for me. So I didn't mind the delays while new cards were put into the game, after she tore hers up.

Sometimes you'll be at a $5 table and someone will sit down and start betting with $100 chips. That happens. But we suggest that you always play where you're not conspicuous with the betting limits you play. It's better to be playing $75 a hand when everyone else is betting $200 than vice-versa. They'll (that is, the floorman and pit boss) be paying attention to the bigger gamblers at the table. If you bet $100 at a $5 table, all eyes will be on you. That's called **heat**, or **drawing the heat**, something you don't need as a skillful player.

All bets must be made prior to the cards being dealt. There will be instances when you can increase your bets by splitting cards or doubling down, which will be explained later. All winning payoffs are even-money, except for payoffs on a blackjack, which are at 3-2.

5

PLAYER'S OPTIONS

INTRODUCTION

As we have seen, the dealer is bound by the house rules and cannot deviate from those rules under any circumstances. For example, suppose you're playing head-to-head with the dealer and you turn over your cards by accident. You're holding a 10-2 for a 12 total. The dealer waits for your decision. You stand, that is, you don't draw any more cards to your hand.

The dealer's upcard is a 6. His hole card is a 10. He has a 16, higher than your 12. If he stood pat, he'd beat you and take away your bet. But the rules of the house state that he must draw to all 16s or below, and so he hits the hand and gets a 9 and busts. You win the bet.

Unlike the dealer, you, as a player, have a number of options available to you. These options are very important and must be taken advantage of in all situations. By using them correctly and intelligently, it's possible to have an advantage over the dealer and thus to win money from the house.

HITTING OR STANDING

A player is dealt two cards to form his original hand. He has the option of either **hitting** the hand, that is, taking one or more cards to improve his total, or standing. By **standing**, he waives the right to get more cards.

We know that hitting the hand is an attempt to improve the point total, but standing is used for two reasons. First of all, the hand might be so strong that drawing a card endangers it by creating a strong opportunity to bust. An example of this might be holding 10-10 for a 20 total. Only one card, an ace, will improve the hand, and every other card in the deck will destroy it by taking it over 21 and busting it. So we'd automatically stand with a 20.

It has been worked out and verified by computer that drawing a card to any total of hard 17 or more creates the same destructive situation. Therefore, with a holding of hard 17 or more, you'll automatically stand with your hand. Note that we're talking about *hard 17* or more. A soft total is quite another thing.

As you recall no hand can be soft without the inclusion of an ace. A soft total is any hand where the ace is counted as an 11, rather than a 1.

Let's assume we hold 10-7. That's a hard 17, and we've stated adamantly that this hand cannot be hit. It can't be hit because there are only four cards that will improve it, the ace, 2, 3 and 4, and nine cards that will destroy it, the 5, 6, 7, 8, 9 and the four 10-value cards.

However, suppose we held an Ace-6. This is a soft 17 with the ace counting as an 11. If we hit this hand, there's no way we can bust it. That's because we can then turn the ace into a 1 and still be below 17. For instance, if we hit

> *We know that the most prevalent card in the deck is a 10, for there are sixteen 10-value cards*

the Ace-6 and got a 10, we'd have a hard 17, with the ace now counting as 1. So there's no way to bust this hand by hitting it.

Let's go back to the option of standing pat. There will be times that we have a rather weak total, but we stand pat anyway, because there may be a strong chance that the dealer will bust his hand. Remember, if we bust first and subsequently the dealer busts, we're still a loser. Therefore, in certain situations we give the dealer the chance to bust first.

Suppose we hold a 10-6, a real **stiff**. Any hard total from 12-16 is known as a **stiff hand**. This is the worst hand we can hold because only five cards can help us, and eight can bust us. Yet, we must hit this hand in certain situations when the dealer holds a 7, 8, 9, 10 or ace. But suppose we see that the dealer's upcard is also a 6. He may hold a 6 or higher as his hole card and thus have a hand valued at 12 or more. If he hits that hand and gets a 10 he'll bust.

We don't know what card he holds as his hole card, for we aren't blessed with X-Ray vision. (Alas, if we were only Superman. We wouldn't have to work at the Daily Planet, we could make a fine living playing blackjack.)

We know that the most prevalent card in the deck is a 10, for there are sixteen 10-value cards, and we have to assume, if the dealer shows a 6 as his upcard, that he may hold another card that gives him a potential bust hand. That's why we'll stand with stiff in certain situations.

For now, we're giving you the theory of standing as against hitting, but in our section on Basic Strategy, we'll cover all hitting and standing strategies.

While we can hit or stand according to best strategy, the dealer is forced to hit or stand according to strict and arbitrary rules of the casino and the game. Thus, this option is of enormous importance to us.

Now for the mechanics of hitting or standing in a blackjack game.

HITTING OR STANDING WHEN CARDS ARE FACE DOWN

In a game where the cards are dealt face down, we lift the cards and hold them in our hand to see their total. If we want to stand, we shove the cards face down under the chips we've already bet.

Single Deck

Hitting   **Standing**

If we want to hit, however, we scrape the cards on the felt surface towards us. If we want another card after the first hit, we scrape them again. We can keep getting cards as long as our total doesn't exceed 21. When we're satisfied with our total, we shove the cards face down under our chips.

What if we've hit and busted the hand? Then we turn over the cards we hold so they're face up. The dealer will verify the count to make certain we've gone over 21, then remove the cards and alas, remove our chips as well.

HITTING OR STANDING WHEN CARDS ARE FACE UP

In games where the cards are dealt out of a shoe, that is, games where four or more decks are used, the cards are generally dealt face up. It's unimportant whether they're face up or down because the dealer can't take advantage of our totals—he's bound by the strict rules of the casino.

When cards are dealt face up, if we stand **pat**, not drawing additional cards, we simply wave one hand palm down over the cards. This is a universal gesture stating that we are standing pat.

If we want to hit the hand, we point a finger, usually the index finger at the cards. This is a universal gesture signifying that we want a hit. We'll keep getting the hand hit as long as our total doesn't exceed 21, if we so desire. What if we bust? It will be obvious to the dealer who sees all our cards. He'll remove them and our bet.

Practice these gestures at home so that by the time you get to a casino you'll look like a seasoned pro.

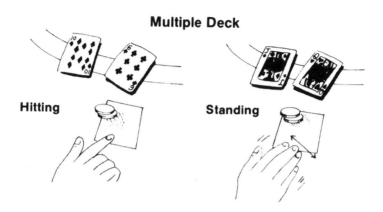

Multiple Deck

Hitting   Standing

DOUBLING DOWN

Doubling down is another important option available to us. There are times when we have the option of doubling our bet before playing out the hand. However, if we do double down, we're restricted to getting only one card to improve the hand. We can't hit more than one.

Let's see how this works in practice.

Let's assume we're dealt a 6-5 for an 11 total. The dealer's upcard is a 6. He has the worst possible upcard, for if he holds a 10 in the hole, he has a very strong chance of busting. Our total of 11 is the best possible total for doubling down. Remember, we can get only one additional card, but if that card is a 10, we can't lose and will most probably win. Not only win, but win at double our original bet.

So we double down. The mechanics are as follows:

DOUBLING DOWN WHEN CARDS ARE DEALT FACE DOWN

In a game where the cards are dealt face down, we turn over our cards and add chips to double the original bet. Suppose we've bet four $5 chips. We place four more $5 chips next to the original bet after turning over our cards. The dealer then knows we're doubling down and will deal us one additional card **face down**. The fact that it's face down means nothing—it's only custom, and we can glance at it immediately if we want to.

If the total of our hand beats the dealer, or if he goes bust, we collect double our original bet. In the example given above, we'd collect $40.

What if we lose? Then we lose the full $40. As we shall find in our Basic Strategy section dealing with doubling down situations, all of our double downs will be to our advantage. We won't win all of them, of course, but we'll win enough to make this option very worthwhile.

Doubling Down

DOUBLING DOWN WHEN CARDS ARE DEALT FACE UP

Now, in casinos where the cards are dealt face up, doubling down is even simpler. We don't ever have to touch our cards when they're dealt face-up. To double down, we simply add chips to our original bet to double their value. Then the dealer will give us a card face up, but he'll place it perpendicular to the two face-up cards.

By the way, when we're in a game where the cards are dealt face down and we've turned them over to double down, the face down card will also be perpendicular to our cards.

MORE ABOUT DOUBLING DOWN

As I've stated, doubling down will be to our advantage in a number of situations. I've spoken to many gamblers in the course of my writing career and some of them, many more than I've realized, don't know anything about correct doubling down. Some never realized that they could double down on any two-card total in Vegas, for example.

Others were superstitious, and told me they always lost when doubling down on certain totals. One woman was adamant about doubling down on 11s. "I never win on that bet," she told me, as if giving me the key to knowledge. I offered to hold a 6-5 or 7-4 and keep doubling down as she ran through the deck, for any amount she wanted to bet. She looked at me blankly and wouldn't take me up on the offer. I told her to go home and try this and if she felt she could still win, I'd be ready to play against her with my 11s. I never heard from her again.

When can you double down? It depends on the jurisdiction or area you're playing in rather than the particular casino. In Southern Nevada, Las Vegas in particular, you can double down on any two cards you hold. In Atlantic City, the same rule applies. In Northern Nevada you can only double down on 10s and 11s held in the original hand. We'll cover these variations as we later discuss various jurisdictions where blackjack is played.

So, remember. You can only double down with the two cards you've originally be dealt. If you don't double down and hit the hand, you can no longer double down. Once you double down, you're only going to get one additional card to form your hand.

SPLITTING PAIRS

Anytime you're dealt identically ranked cards, you have the option to **split** them and play them as two separate hands. This means that your original bet will now double, since you must put down a bet equal to that bet on the split card. Let's see how this works.

Suppose you're dealt 8-8. You can split them by separating them. If you're in a game where the cards are dealt face down, you turn them over, separate the cards and put down an additional bet equal to your original one. If you're in a game where the cards are dealt face up, you simply separate the cards and make an additional bet on the separated card.

Now that you've separated the two 8s, you play them as original hands. Let's assume that with the first original 8 you hit and get a 6. Now you have a 14 on the first hand. Let's say you hit that hand again and get a 10. You've gone over 21 and busted, and therefore the cards on that hand and the chips are taken away by the dealer.

Now you play the second hand. Let's assume that you hit and get an ace. You now have a soft 19, a strong hand and decide to stand. If you beat the dealer with that total or the dealer busts, you win that bet.

Splitting Pairs

As we mentioned, you can split any cards of equal rank. You can split 2-2, 3-3, 4-4, and so forth. Any 10-value cards are considered of equal rank. Thus, if you're dealt a king and a jack, you an split them as 10s. This is not to say that all pairs should be split. As we shall see in our Basic Strategy chapter, we should never split 5s or 10s.

Some players think that if they've been dealt a pair, they should split them. This is a terrible and losing strategy. Only certain pairs should be split

> *You can split any cards of equal rank: 2-2, 3-3, 4-4, and so forth, but you should never split 5s or 10s.*

45

against certain dealer's upcards. Splitting pairs occurs much less often than doubling down, but it can be very profitable if done correctly.

Most casinos, with the exception of the Atlantic City houses, will permit you to resplit pairs.

For example, if you've split 9s and get another 9 on either 9 split, you can resplit it. Suppose you play out the first 9 and get a 5 and stand with a hard 14. On the second 9 you get another 9. You can now resplit this 9 by putting out another bet equal to your original wager. If you get yet another 9, you can again resplit it.

SPLITTING ACES

A separate rule applies to the splitting of aces. If you split them, you're only allowed one additional card to be dealt to each ace, and if you get an ace on an ace, you can't resplit the aces. There are a few casinos that allow you to resplit aces, but none that I know that allow you more than one card on an ace that is split.

DOUBLING DOWN AFTER SPLITTING

Here we combine doubling down and splitting of pairs. It works this way: Suppose you're dealt a pair of 8s and you split them, putting out a separate bet on each 8. On the first 8, which you hit, you're dealt a 3. Now you have an 11, and in some casinos, you're permitted to **double down after splitting** so now you can double your bet on this hand, and receive one additional card to your 8-3.

Doubling down after splitting is offered in a number of casinos and is of enormous advantage to a player, especially a skilled card counter. Yet many players are ignorant of the fact that they may be playing in a casino that allows this option.

Always ask, when you sit down at a blackjack table, just what options are allowed, and particularly if you can double down after splitting pairs. Not only can you double down on the first split hand, as shown in the example above, but if you're dealt a 2 or 3 on the next 8, you can double down that hand as well.

I've been involved in a game where I split 8s in a single deck game, and where the dealer's upcard was a 5, a bad card for her, as we shall see in basic strategy. Since basic strategy states that 8s must be split against any upcard, it has even more profitable significance when split against the 5. So I split the 8s, and received a 3 on the first 8. I doubled down, and received a card face down. I then hit the other 8 and got another 8, which I split. I received a 2 on the second 8 and doubled that down. I received another 2 on the third 8 and doubled that down.

> *Always ask, when you sit down at a blackjack table, just what options are allowed, and particularly if you can double down after splitting pairs.*

Having bet $100 on the original hand, I now had $600 in bets on the three doubled-down hands, all as a result of originally splitting 8s. The dealer turned over her hole card, which was a 10, and hit her 15 and got another 10 and busted. So I won $600 on my original $100 bet.

If you study Basic Strategy you'll see when it pays to double down after splitting. Any valid double-down of a particular total applies also to the double down after splitting. For example, if it pays to double down a 10 or 11 against a dealer's 5, it certainly pays to double down the same total after splitting.

Doubling down after splitting is allowed in several Nevada casinos, particularly in Las Vegas, as well as in all Atlantic City casinos.

INSURANCE

The insurance bet is the most misunderstood of all the player's options. Most dealers don't know the proper time to take insurance, and often will misdirect the player in this regard.

When the dealer shows an ace as his upcard, he will ask the players if they want **insurance**. He makes this request before peeking at his hole card. What he really is asking the players is this—do they want to bet that he has a blackjack? If he has one, the players win the insurance bet at 2-1. If he doesn't have a10 in the hole, he collects all the insurance bets, which are now losers, and the game goes on.

Insurance pays 2-1, but the player is limited to half his original wager as an insurance bet. For example, if you've made a $50 bet prior to the cards being dealt out, and wish to make an insurance bet, you're limited to a $25 wager.

If you win the insurance bet, this means that the dealer has a blackjack, and so you lose your original bet. But since you're paid $50 at 2-1 on your $25 insurance wager, and lose your $50 original wager, it's a wash.

If you didn't make the insurance bet, and the dealer has a blackjack, you'd lose your original $50 bet. However, if you lose your insurance bet, you still have to play out your hand, and may lose that also, causing you to drop 1 1/2 times your original bet.

Suppose you hold a 10-2 and the dealer shows an ace. He asks if you want to take insurance. You have your original $50 wager on the table, and now shove out a $25 chip as your insurance wager. The dealer peeks at his hole card and then snatches away your insurance bet. He doesn't have a blackjack. So far you're down $25 on this hand and now have to hit the 10-2. You get a 10 and bust and end up losing $75.

INSURING YOUR OWN BLACKJACK?

Dealers and casino employees always tell players that they should insure their blackjack. What they mean is this—if a dealer shows an ace, and the player himself is holding a blackjack, he should take the insurance bet. Why? Dealers explain that "you can't lose. Either way you're going to win your original bet." Well, that's true. Here's how it works.

You still have your original $50 bet out and you peek and see you have a blackjack, but damn! The dealer is showing an ace, and he might have one also. If you don't make the insurance bet and the dealer has a blackjack, then all you'll get is a push—blackjack vs. blackjack and no one wins.

If you do "insure your blackjack" by putting out $25 as an insurance bet, you're guaranteed a $50 payout, equal to your original wager. If the dealer has a blackjack, your blackjack is a push, but he pays you 2-1 on the insurance bet and you collect $50.

If the dealer doesn't have a [blackjack], he takes away your $25 insurance bet, but pays you $75 for your $50 bet at 3-2. So you net $50 either way.

Well, if that's the case, are these dealers correct in insisting that you "insure your black-jacks?" No. What the bet really boils down to is this. When you

Unless you're a card counter and know what the count is, you shouldn't take insurance.

make the insurance wager, what you're betting is that the dealer has a blackjack. Instead of insurance, the dealer should really ask, "who wants to bet that I have a black-jack?" For that's what this wager is all about.

Unless you've learned to count cards and know what the count is, you shouldn't take insurance. Even if you have a blackjack yourself, you should avoid the bet. Let's see why with a very simple example.

Let's assume you've sat down at an empty table, and the dealer had dealt you one hand after you've bet $10. You see that you have a blackjack. Great! But the dealer shows an ace, and he says to you "insurance?" Well, do you take it? Do you make a $5 wager that he has black-jack?

Let's examine the situation mathematically.

There are three cards that you have seen, two aces and a 10. In the deck are sixteen 10s and thirty six other cards. This means that of the cards you don't know, fifteen are 10s and thirty-four are other cards, cards that won't form the dealer's blackjack.

If you make the bet, you're getting 2-1 on a bet that should really net you 34-15, and that gives the house about an 8% edge. So it isn't worth making the bet.

Remember, most of the time the deck will be so constructed that the odds are against the dealer holding a blackjack when he shows an ace. Only when the deck has at least enough 10s to bring the ratio down to 2-1 in terms of other cards vs. 10s, is it worthwhile making the insurance wager.

In some casinos where the insurance bet is allowed, the dealer won't peek at his hole card till after all the players have acted upon their hands. They make the insurance bet immediately, but then play out their hands and finally the dealer peeks at his hole card. If he has a blackjack, then those players making the insurance bet get 2-1, and the others lose their original wagers. Note that we said *original wagers*. If a player doubles down or splits cards and adds to his original total, and it turns out that the dealer has a 10 in addition to his ace upcard, those additional bets will be returned to the player. He or she only loses the original bet.

Some players are afraid to double down or split when they see a dealer's ace in these instances, afraid they're going to lose double their bet, but that's not the case at all.

INSURANCE BET SUMMARIZED

The insurance wager is generally bad for the player. There will be times when it is worthwhile, but only when a player is counting cards and knows that the ratio of other cards to 10s is 2-1 or less. In our section on Counting Cards, we'll show when this occurs.

EARLY SURRENDER

This option was once standard in Atlantic City, where it was known as **Early Surrender**. A player could surrender half his bet and give up his cards *before* the dealer checked to see if he had a blackjack, when holding an ace or 10 as his upcard.

Why would a player surrender half his original bet without giving himself the chance to improve his hand? The player may feel that he will lose his entire original bet if he acts on his hand, either standing or hitting it. Suppose he holds a 10-6 and the dealer has an ace showing. There's a good possibility that the player will bust if he hits his hand, and lose if he doesn't hit it. The ace is a very powerful card in the dealer's hand—there are a lot of ways he can get up to 17 and stand and beat the player. So, in this instance, the player gives up half his bet rather than taking the chance of losing it all.

But now all this is rather moot in A.C. The casinos there have given up the early surrender option.

SURRENDER

The more conventional Surrender or Late Surrender can still be found in casinos. Here, there can be no surrender till the dealer is assured that he doesn't have a blackjack. This cuts down on the effectiveness of surrender, because the dealer's ace or 10 may lead to a blackjack, and there will be times when the player won't be able to surrender because the dealer has an immediate blackjack.

Surrender can still be an effective option and we'll cover it in our Basic Strategy and Counting Cards sections.

The mechanics of surrender are simple. If you've been dealt cards face down, you turn them over, place them on the table and say "surrender." Half your bet and the cards will be taken away by the dealer.

If you receive your cards face up, simply say " surrender." Let the dealer remove half the chips. Don't touch your chips after you've made a bet. Your cards, of course, will also be taken away by the dealer.

RAISING OR LOWERING BETS

This is a player's option that isn't often thought of as a separate option. However, it is of utmost importance. Unlike other games, such as craps, roulette and baccarat, where a player will move his bet either upward or downward according to a whim or hunch, or a mistaken belief that he is in the "middle of a winning streak," in blackjack, there will be a definite reason for raising or lowering a bet.

The reason is this—if the cards are favorable to the player, the bet will be increased and if the cards are unfavorable to the player, the bet will be reduced. There is logic in this. In a game like craps, where what happened before has no bearing on what happens next, raising or lowering a bet means nothing unless luck is on the side of the gambler. But it means a great deal in blackjack, where luck will eventually even itself out, and where the mathematical knowledge of the favorability or unfavorability of the cards is a certainty.

How does one know when the deck is favorable or unfavorable? By card counting. This doesn't mean keeping track of every card in the deck. We're going to deal with an effective and simple method of counting that will give you a clear idea of where the cards stand. Armed with that knowledge, we're going to show you how to take full advantage of this to either increase or decrease your wagers. There will be times when you will keep the same wager. All this will be thoroughly gone into at the appropriate time in Card Counting.

For now, know that when you raise or lower your bets, you'll have logic behind the moves and they will always be to your advantage.

PLAYER'S OPTIONS - ADVANTAGES

All of the player's options mentioned in this chapter are to the advantage of the player when exercised correctly.

By this statement we mean that just exercising options without rhyme or reason will work to the disadvantage of the player. For example, we showed that "insuring a blackjack" off the top of the deck gives the house an 8% advantage. At other times, however, the insurance bet will favor the player.

As we shall see in the chapter on Basic Strategy, the proper use of options will make money for the player. These are the chief tools he has.

> *All of the player's options mentioned in this chapter are to your advantage when exercised correctly.*

If it weren't for the fact that the player could double down, split cards, take insurance and in some instances, surrender, the game would be a negative one, always favoring the house.

Therefore, what the player will want to use is the judicious raising and lowering of his bets. If he raises his bets in favorable situations, he will win more, and if he lowers his bets in unfavorable situations, he will lose less. Taken together, they will almost guarantee that the player will end up a winner in the long run.

6

CASINO RULES

INTRODUCTION

In this next chapter we're going to examine the casino rules as they affect play in various jurisdictions. Rules can be divided into two categories—those that are standard, and those that are optional in certain jurisdictions, or at casinos within a particular area. For example, in Las Vegas, there are two distinct sections, the Strip and Downtown, both with different rules.

Standard Rules

- Hitting and Standing
- Raising and Lowering of Bets
- Blackjack pays 6-5 or 3-2
- Ties are pushes
- Pairs may be split
- Doubling down is permitted
- Insurance pays 2-1

All of the above rules, which include some player's options, are favorable to the player. With these options, the game is almost an even one between players and the house. With the next set of optional rules, we'll see how each option favors or hurts the player.

OPTIONAL RULES - ADVANTAGES AND DISADVANTAGES

Some of these are favorable to the player, while others are unfavorable. If favorable, we'll express it as a "+," if unfavorable as a "-."

The figures shown are the percentages each rule is favorable or unfavorable. Note that each option gives or takes away a small percentage, none more than 6/10 of 1%. Even though rules may give the house a small advantage, this advantage is off the top of the deck. With patience, card counting and correct betting strategies, we can easily overcome any minor starting disadvantages.

Effect of Rules Changes	
• Doubling down on only 10s and 11s only	- .28
• Dealer must hit soft 17	- .20
• Dealer stands on all 17s	+ .20
• Early surrender allowed	+ .60
• Conventional surrender allowed	+ .01
• Doubling down after splitting pairs allowed	+ .12
• Resplitting of aces	+ .03
• No resplitting of pairs	- .05
• Two decks in play	- .40
• Four decks in play	- .50
• Six decks in play	- .60
• No insurance allowed	- .40
• Blackjack pays only 6 to 5	-1.40

RULES BY JURISDICTION

In this section, we'll deal with the major jurisdictions, Las Vegas, Northern Nevada (Reno and Lake Tahoe), Atlantic City and the riverboats. As more and more gambling venues come on board, such as more riverboats plying the Mississippi, Indian reservation blackjack, and New Orleans and other big cities legalizing gambling, use this chapter as your guide. Study the rules allowed and then add up or subtract the various optional rules to see just what the starting advantage or disadvantage you face as a player.

First we'll deal with Las Vegas, which is divided into two parts, the **Strip** and **Downtown**. The Strip contains many luxurious hotels and also includes hotels nearby though not on the Strip itself, that use Strip rules.

LAS VEGAS STRIP

Four deck blackjack games and six deck games are the standard. There are single deck games offered as well, but you'll have to check on current conditions as casino offerings constantly change. What is in vogue this year may be out the next. A relatively new rule, which works to the player's disadvantage, is the reduced payout of only 6 to 5 on a player's blackjack, as opposed to the expected 2 to 1, which had been the standard for decades. This is a terrible rule that costs you 1.4% in a single deck game (slightly less in multiple deck games), so you'll always want to play in games paying 2 to 1 on blackjacks, where possible.

The Strip follows all the standard rules we've previously shown, and among the optional rules, two are common to all Strip casinos. These are:

Standard Rules
- Doubling down on any two cards
- Dealer stands on all 17s

Other optional rules depend on the whim of the particular casino you're playing in. Some have conventional surrender, others don't offer any surrender. In some casinos, you can double down after splitting pairs, in others this option is not available.

The first thing you should do when playing on the Strip is ask the dealer just what rules are in force at his table. He may give you a limited answer, so you will want to specifically ask if there is surrender, if you're permitted to double down after splitting pairs, and just how many decks he's dealing from the shoe. Armed with this information, you'll have a much clearer picture of what the game offers.

For example, suppose the following optional rules are in effect:

- Six decks   - .60
- Doubling down after pair splitting   + .12

Our disadvantage is -.48. Perhaps we could go across the street to another casino where there are only four-deck games, bringing our disadvantage to -.38. Or we might find a two-deck game, lowering the disadvantage to -.28.

This disadvantage is just off the top of the deck. With

card counting and judicious raising and lowering of bets we can overcome this small disadvantage and come out winners. With multiple deck games there may be long stretches of favorability. We must take advantage of this with larger bets. With equally long stretches of unfavorable cards, we must make minimum bets.

The important thing to remember is this—all Strip casinos are not created equal. Try and find the best game for yourself with the best rules in force. There are plenty of casinos out on the Strip, ranging from the gaudy superstars down to casinos adjacent to rinkydink motels. Find the one that suits you best, with the rules that are best for you.

And most importantly, ask what the rules are before sitting down. We can't stress this enough.

LAS VEGAS DOWNTOWN

The downtown section of Vegas offers all sorts of games. You can play at tourist places such as the Golden Nugget, or "local" spots such as El Cortez or Lady Luck, or at the unique Horseshoe Club, which attracts both tourists and locals, small-timers and big players.

If single deck games are readily available, then it would be foolish to play any other game, such as double deck or multiple deck games. You're just putting extra obstacles in your path towards winning.

Why give up either -.40, -.50 or -.60 when you don't have to.

The Following are Typical Downtown Rules:

Typical Downtown Rules
- All standard rules
- Single deck game to four deck games
- Dealer hits soft 17
- Doubling down on any two cards

This leaves the player with a slight disadvantage of -.20 in a single deck game because of the soft 17 rule. But it's going to be difficult to find any downtown casino which has single deck games and a rule that forces the dealer to stand on all 17s.

Also, as mentioned earlier, the 6 to 5 payouts on blackjack are very costly to the tune of 1.4%, so you'll want to avoid those games entirely. That's a big disadvantage, especially if the game is multiple deck. Actually, experienced blackjack players consider the 6 to 5 games to be sucker plays and they would never sit down at a table offering those rules.

In a 4 deck game the disadvantage moves to -.70. Therefore it pays to play the single deck game when playing downtown. There are plenty of these games available and an astute player should take advantage of them.

Even though the Strip has the reputation of attracting the high rollers, with its fancier structures and rooms, there is plenty of room for big action downtown.

CARDOZA PUBLISHING • EDWIN SILBERSTANG

NORTHERN NEVADA

The casinos in Lake Tahoe and Reno offer a great many single-deck games. That shouldn't be a problem for you. However, a couple of rules are negative for the player. Here's what to expect in Northern Nevada.

The Following are Typical Northern Nevada Rules:

Typical Northern Nevada Rules
- All standard rules
- Single deck game
- Double down only on 10s and 11s
- Dealer hits soft 17

Those two features, doubling down on 10s and 11s only and the dealer hitting soft 17s, gives the casinos there an initial advantage of .48 over the player.

ATLANTIC CITY

Unlike other jurisdictions, where rules may change from casino to casino and even within a casino, in A.C. all rules are standard, formulated by the Gaming Commission of New Jersey. The only possible variation is the number of decks the casino will play with, either two, four or six.

Here's what to expect on the Atlantic Ocean coast of New Jersey.

The Following are Typical Atlantic City Rules:

> ## Typical Atlantic City Rules
> • All standard rules
> • Six decks
> • Double down on any two cards
> • Double down after splitting pairs
> • No resplitting of pairs
> • Dealer stands on all 17s

This works out to a -.33 for the player. At one time Atlantic City had early surrender, but the greed of card counters who trumpeted their huge wins there, killed that option. If possible, play at a four deck game rather than a six deck game for the slighter advantage it affords you. If you can find a two deck game, even better.

THE RIVERBOATS

Use the rules below as a general guide. Since riverboats are governed by individual state laws, they may have different rules as well as betting limits.

Again, as with other jurisdictions, study the rules before playing.

The Following are Typical Riverboat Rules:

> ## Typical Riverboat Rules
> • All standard rules
> • Doubling down - any two cards
> • Multiple deck games: 4-6 decks

INDIAN RESERVATIONS

The Following are Typical Indian Rules:

Typical Indian Reservation Rules
- All standard rules
- Four to Six Decks
- Double down on any two cards

The above rules may change from state to state. Use these rules as a general guide.

EUROPEAN RULES

The Following are Typical European Rules:

Typical European Rules
- Dealer hits all 16s and stands on all 17s.
- Insurance is allowed when dealer shows an ace.
- Insurance pays 2-1.
- A blackjack pays 3-2
- Doubling down only on 9, 10 or 11.
- Dealer doesn't deal himself a hole card till all players have acted.
- Most games are four or six decks.
- If player draws a 2 on A-8 after doubling, the total counts as 11, not 21.
- Tipping may not be permitted.
- Spectators can also participate in a player's hand by making a bet,and are subject to the player's decisions.

ASIA-CARIBBEAN-OTHER LOCATIONS

The European rules are the most prevalent around the world. However, various countries may have their own unique rules. Don't expect to find single deck games, however. And always ask what the prevailing rules are before sitting down and playing.

If there are too many restrictions so that the game is very unfavorable to the player, pass.

UNUSUAL RULES

Sometimes you run into an odd rule in a casino. I was waiting for a friend to show up at a Strip hotel south of Flamingo Road when I noticed a single deck game nearby. Since all the other games there were six decks, I sat down, cashed in a couple of hundred dollars and started playing. I was ahead by a few dollars when the deck became favorable and I was dealt an Ace-6 against the dealer's 6. I turned over the cards to double down, but the dealer, an Oriental woman, informed me that I could only do so on 10 or 11.

"What do you mean? All the other games here allow doubling down on any two cards." A floorman materialized. He told me this was a special rule for the one single deck game they offered. So I hit the hand, and won a single instead of a double, bet.

I left the game right away and cashed in. I was *steaming* and didn't want to play when angry. And I could always get a better single deck game downtown. My friend came and as we drove away, I noticed the marquee advertising in big blue letters "Single Deck Blackjack." What a charade!

THE 495 POUND ACE!

But then, there are those odd rules that suddenly come up and benefit a player. I was with a friend in a West End casino in London, filled with heavy smoke and a dreary atmosphere. Most of the action centered on two roulette wheels, where gamblers gathered around, excitedly making bets.

We headed for the blackjack tables in the rear. There were three altogether, two full and one empty. So I sat down at the empty table, with my friend watching. He was anxious to see me in action, having read several of my gambling books and novels.

The dealer was a young woman who had a rather sad looking face. Something personal must have been bothering her, for despite her wan smile to us, she looked distracted. Her mind was definitely somewhere else.

I had a good run at the table, and was ahead a couple of hundred pounds after a few deals. I was ready to go when the decks got very favorable, and I had a +4 true count with only about a deck to go. I was now betting ten units of five pound chips, and won my last hand. The deck was still +4, and now the dealer dealt me a hard 17, 10-7 while she showed a 10 as her upcard.

I stood pat, and she now dealt herself a 3 for a 13, then a 4 for a hard 17. She had to stand, but distracted, she slid another card out of the shoe, an ace, and was about to add it to her total when I pointed out that she already had a 17. I wanted a push, not a loss.

"I'm terribly sorry, luv," she said, and bewildered, she looked around for her supervisor, a middle-aged man with a brightly checkered vest. He came over, the situation was explained to him, and he told her that her 17 was a push with mine. As to the ace?

"The player gets the ace next hand," he said, and strolled away. I couldn't believe this. In America, the ace would be burned and put out of play. But here they were allowing me to receive it, which meant that one of my cards was guaranteed now, and the deck even more favorable.

I hesitated for a moment, while she gathered in the played cards, and shoved all of my chips, 330 pounds, into the betting box.

I expected her to call the floorman again, or say something about my bet, but she just slid the ace over to me, showed me her 9 as an upcard, and gave me the jack of diamonds for a blackjack. I had won £495, at a time when the pound was £1.30 to a dollar. On one hand.

I wanted to toke her but she told me tips weren't permitted, so I thanked her and went and cashed out. That night I treated my friend to a sumptuous Indian dinner and the theater, taking her to Les Miserables, which had just opened with the Royal Shakespeare Company performing the musical. A jolly good night on London town.

That London episode was a lucky one for me. However, I've passed up games on ships and in other countries when the rules were unfavorable, giving me little chance of winning.

When you're on a ship or in a foreign land, and you have a chance to play blackjack, ask about the rules. It is important to know what you're in for before you start putting your money on the table.

Use our book as a guide, and you'll know just where you stand in terms of favorability or unfavorability. Only if you find the game to be good, play. Otherwise, see the sights somewhere else.

7

SINGLE DECK BASIC STRATEGY

INTRODUCTION

Basic Strategy means **basic winning strategy**. All plays covered in this chapter are correct plays, and must be made for a player to have a winning chance. A player can't afford to play hunches or feelings when playing blackjack if he or she expects to come out ahead. There are correct plays that must be followed exactly.

For now, we're covering basic strategy without the effect of counting cards, which will change some of the moves shown. Forget about card counting at this point, and concentrate on correct play as shown in Basic Strategy.

I meet a lot of players, some of whom seek me out, and want to tell me their blackjack stories, most of which are tedious and boring. A great many of these stories have to do with going against correct strategy on some wild hunch and how it paid off. They don't tell me about the hunches that destroyed their bankrolls; those are conveniently forgotten.

And a number of players tell me that they're losers despite "knowing the game." All I have to do is ask a couple of simple questions to see how little they really know about blackjack.

The first question I always ask is this: "You're at a blackjack table and the dealer shows a 7 as his upcard. You're holding an ace and a 6. What do you do?"

It's amazing how many players who gamble with really serious money don't know the answer to this question. They stare at me and think about the situation. They have 17 and the dealer has 17. It's a push. Why risk hitting the hand? I can see their mental processes working. Some say they stand pat; others, thinking it's a trick question needing an expert reply, say they'll double down!

Both answers are wrong, of course. When you hold a soft 17 (Ace-6) against a dealer's 7, the correct play is to hit.

Having asked that question and gotten a strange answer, I now ask, "suppose you have the same Ace-6, and the dealer shows a 3. What do you do?" There's more thinking going on. The answers are usually divided between standing and hitting, and yet the correct move is to double down here!

The point of this digression is this—you should know basic strategy cold before playing blackjack for money. Every move should be memorized, so that not only will you give a correct answer immediately, but more importantly, when faced with the situation in actual play, you'll make the right move.

In this chapter we're not only going to give you the correct strategy but tell you the reason for the strategy.

Furthermore, we're going to divide the strategies between soft totals and hard totals, and give the correct play for each group, in all situations.

> **All plays shown in the charts are correct plays, and must be made for you to have a winning chance.**

We're also going to divide the strategies for maximum efficiency into those for **Hitting vs. Standing**, **Splitting Pairs** and **Doubling Down**, and then we're going to combine them all into one **Master Strategy**.

The following symbols will be used throughout the strategy tables:

```
H   = Hit
S   = Stand
DBL = Double Down
SP  = Split
```

In all our charts, the dealer's upcard is indicated by the horizontal numbers, (running left to right) on the top row, and the player's hand is indicted by the vertical numbers (up and down) in the left column. The letters in the matrix indicate the correct strategy play.

SINGLE DECK HITTING VS. STANDING

	2	3	4	5	6	7	8	9	10	A
	Single Deck Hitting vs. Standing									
	Hard Totals									
11/less	H	H	H	H	H	H	H	H	H	H
12	H	H	S	S	S	H	H	H	H	H
13	S	S	S	S	S	H	H	H	H	H
14	S	S	S	S	S	H	H	H	H	H
15	S	S	S	S	S	H	H	H	H	H
16	S	S	S	S	S	H	H	H	H	H
17-21	S	S	S	S	S	S	S	S	S	S

H = Hit   **S** = Stand

Study the chart and practice till you know every play by heart. This is the core of basic strategy, and until you master hitting vs. standing strategy, you shouldn't play for real money in a casino.

HARD 12 VS. DEALER 2-3

Players holding a hard 12 against a dealer's 2 or 3 seem to be lost if they don't know or understand basic strategy. Sometimes they stand and sometimes they hit. They often tell me, "I always bust when I hit a hard 12." That's far from true. Only a 10 will bust them, and any other card will not.

Since it's the most difficult stiff hand for a player to bust with, it should be hit against the dealer's 2 or 3. We're assuming that the dealer holds a 10 as a hole card, and of his stiff hands, these are the most difficult for him to bust. By **stiff hands**, we mean any hand from hard 12 to hard 16 that, if hit, is in danger of busting.

HARD 12 VS. DEALER 4-6, 7-A

If a dealer has a 4-6, then the player stands on his hard 12, allowing the dealer first crack at busting. If the dealer shows a 7-Ace, the hard 12 will be hit until the player gets at least a 17, then he'll stand. Thus, if the dealer shows a 9, and the player gets a 4 on his 10-2, he'll hit again according to the chart. Now that he has a hard 16, he hits against the dealer's 10.

HARD 13-16

When we hold a stiff total of 13-16, we're most at risk of busting. Therefore we stand against any dealer's stiff card (2-6) but hit against a 7-Ace.

HARD 17 OR HIGHER

With the hard 17 or higher, we never hit. We are in danger of busting too often, and it's a losing play.

SINGLE DECK - SPLITTING PAIRS

Many players believe that if they're dealt a pair, it should be split. You'll see this quite often at blackjack tables, with players splitting everything that pairs, with no regard to the favorability of the move. We must be more discerning in our pair splitting. Only certain pairs should be split against certain upcards, and some pairs should never be split. Conversely, there are pairs that should always be split.

SPLITTING 2-2

Now, let's examine the rationale for pair splitting. Our 2-2 gives us a total of four, which is worse than an individual card totaling 2, so, against the 3-7, we split. If we hit an individual 2 and get a 6-9, we've significantly improved the hand. Against the dealer's 2, we don't split, because the 2 gives him many ways to make his hand. So we hit the hand, as we do against a dealer's 8-Ace, and hope for the best.

If we hit the 2-2, which is a hard 4, we follow the rules of the previous table on Hitting and Standing, and play accordingly, depending on what the dealer's upcard is. For example, if the dealer's upcard was an 8, we keep hitting until we have at least a hard 17, then stand.

SINGLE DECK SPLITTING PAIRS
No Doubling After Splitting

	2	3	4	5	6	7	8	9	10	A
22		spl	spl	spl	spl	spl				
33			spl	spl	spl	spl				
44										
55										
66	spl	spl	spl	spl	spl					
77	spl	spl	spl	spl	spl	spl			*	
88	spl	spl	spl	spl	spl	spl	spl	spl	spl	spl
99	spl	spl	spl	spl	spl		spl	spl		
10-10										
AA	spl	spl	spl	spl	spl	spl	spl	spl	spl	spl

H = Hit   **S** = Stand   **D** = Double   **spl** = Split

*Actually a stand situation in single deck. See Splitting 77

SPLITTING 3-3

The 3-3 gives us a possible foundation of 6, which, together with a 10, forms our worst hand of 16. So we're anxious to break up the 3s against a 4-7 dealer's upcard. We don't split against a dealer's 2 or 3 because our individual 3 here can quickly be busted with the addition of two 10s. We prefer to play out our bad 6 for one loss, rather than splitting for two losses. The same reasoning holds true when we face a dealer's 8-Ace.

SPLITTING 4-4

The 4-4 gives us an 8 total, which is much stronger than individual 4s, so we don't split it, no matter what the dealer's upcard. If we get a 10 to the 4-4, we have an 18, a reasonable, but not a very strong hand. Still, it's better than splitting the 4s, getting a 10, then an 8 and busting the first hand, then running into the same problem with the second split 4, resulting in a double loss.

SPLITTING 5-5

The 5-5 presents a different situation. It forms a 10, a very strong total, whereas splitting the 5s give us two weak foundation cards, susceptible to busting. With the 5-5, as we shall see in the table on Doubling Down, we will double down most of the time with this holding.

SPLITTING 6-6

6-6 should be split against a dealer's 2-6. Even though we have two weak foundation cards in individual 6s by splitting, we're only splitting against a dealer's stiff card, of 2-6. We make this play more to limit losses than to increase our winnings. Against a dealer's 7-Ace, we hit our 6-6, which is a hard 12, and hope we don't get a 10 to bust our hand.

SPLITTING 7-7

7-7 is split against a 2-7, with the expectation that a 7 base will form a 17 if we hit a 10, and sometimes will be even a higher total. We only take the chance of splitting against a 2-7, and not an 8 or 9, for example, since two 17s might give us a double loss against a dealer's 18 or 19.

7-7 VS. DEALER 10

Note the * on the 7 against the 10. We stand with two 7s against a 10. The reasoning is this. We are playing a single deck game and already have two 7s. Only another 7 will beat a dealer's potential 20, and the chances of this happening have been diminished considerably. So we stand.

SPLITTING 8-8

8s are always split. Together they form a 16, a horrible total, one that is in most danger of being busted. But separately, we have individual bases of 8, which isn't bad. A 10 to the 8 gives us 18 and a fighting chance to push or win. Again, this move is made to diminish overall losses rather than as an aggressive winning move. The more we cut down on losses, the more it'll add up in wins in the long run.

SPLITTING 9-9

The two 9s are best split against all cards from the 2 through the 9, with the exception of the 7. Why don't we split against the 7? Simple. Two 9s give us 18. The dealer's 7 gives him a potential 17. We have a winner and we don't tamper with it.

Splitting the 9s gives us a good shot at a double win especially against the dealer's stiff cards of 3-6, and it is just slightly favorable against the dealer's 2. Against the dealer's 8, we're trying for a double win instead of a push, if we hit 10s on each 9. Against the 9, we're trying to avoid one loss (our 18 to the dealer's 19) by hoping for a 10 on each 9 we split.

Very few players split the 9s correctly. They're afraid to split against the dealer's 8 or 9, but those are great moves. I've won a lot of money making them, usually to the disgusted looks of other "big players," who really knew very little about the fine points of the game.

SPLITTING 10-10

Two 10s, that is, any 10-value cards, give us a 20 hard total, very very strong. If you were always guaranteed a 20, without being dealt any cards, and let the dealer deal to himself and play out hands, you'd be a millionaire in no time. Don't split them.

Be satisfied with the 20.

There may be times, as you understand card counting and advanced strategy, that you'll be tempted to split the 10s in certain rare situations. But even if they're favorable, it's such an unusual move that you'll draw heat, that is, casino scrutiny and countermeasures.

At various tables I've seen people split 10s, but they weren't skilled players, just fools, ready to part with theri money. I've seen one take a deck that was just perfect, full of 10s, and split and resplit it down to the bottom, till he ended up with six losers. There's nothing you can do in situations like that except leave the table before you strangle the idiot.

SPLITTING ACE-ACE

Aces should always be split. Each ace gives you a foundation of 11, the best possible base from which to get a hit. A 10 gives you a no-lose hand. So, no matter what the dealer is holding as his upcard, split the aces. It's an even better play at a casino where you can resplit aces, a rare treat for players. I once resplit till I had four aces out, and was dealt two 10s, a 9 and an 8.

The dealer's upcard was a 7, and he held a 10 as his hole card.

Serendipity!!!

SINGLE DECK DOUBLING DOWN

SINGLE DECK DOUBLING DOWN Hard Totals										
	2	3	4	5	6	7	8	9	10	A
62										
44/53				D	D					
9	D	D	D	D	D					
10	D	D	D	D	D	D	D	D		
11	D	D	D	D	D	D	D	D	D	D

D = Double Down   **Blank** = Hit, Do Not Double Down

DOUBLING 11

An 11 is the best of the double-down hands a player can have. With an 11, any 10 gives the player a 21, a probable winner—the best the dealer can do is push. The 10s are the most prevalent cards in the deck, so no matter what card the dealer shows, an 11 is a profitable double.

As a fine point, a 6-5 is the best of the 11s you can hold for doubling down, for the 5 and 6 give you two cards you don't want remaining in the deck. A 9-2 is the worst, since you have a 9 in your hand rather than in the deck, and a 9 to an 11 gives you a 20. This doesn't alter the situation however. No matter how your 11 is composed, double down against any dealer's upcard.

DOUBLING 10

With the 10, the situation changes slightly. Since a 10 added to a 10 total gives you a 20, it is not possible to double down safely against a dealer's 10 or ace. Against the dealer's 10, you're taking a big chance, for the best you may get is an ace for a 21. That's a real longshot. More probably, you'll be dealt a 10 on your 10 for a 20. If the dealer holds 10 as his upcard, there's a strong possibility that he already has a 20, so you're doubling your bet in the hope of getting a push. Not a good move.

If the dealer holds an ace as his upcard, doubling down with a 10 is also a bad move, especially if the dealer hits soft 17, where he can make all kinds of hands.

DOUBLING 9

The 9 is much weaker than the 10 or 11 for doubling down purposes, so you won't double down against any card higher than a dealer's 6.

DOUBLING 8

The 8 is the weakest of all double down totals. It should be tried only against the dealer's 5 or 6, and only when you're holding a 4-4 or 5-3.

DOUBLING 7 OR LESS

Other than these hard totals, you don't double down. A 7 is useless as a double down total, and will lose much more than it will win. You want to hit a 7 or weaker hard total in the hopes of improving to a hand of 17 or higher.

MORE ON DOUBLING

Remember, when doubling down, you're limited to just one card. If that card is a dud, you're out of luck unless the dealer busts. For example, if you double down on 11 and get an ace, you're in big trouble, especially if the dealer holds a 7 or higher card. You now have to pray that he busts and you've already doubled your original bet.

I've seen the craziest doubling downs in my career as a blackjack player and observer of the game. I have already mentioned the Chinese woman who played with cash out of a paper bag, and tore up her cards when the dealer dealt herself a blackjack.

LUCKY EDDIE BOY

On one hand, the Chinese woman put out $1,800 as her bet and she looked over her cards carefully. I was sitting next to her and saw that she held an 8-4. The dealer's upcard was a 9. The lady turned the cards over and announced she was doubling down. She started pulling cash out of her bag. "You've got a 12," I said.

"I know, I know, Eddie boy. I know I got a 12, but if you don't like to gamble, you don't play 21. I double down. I feel lucky. You make me feel lucky, Eddie boy."

So the dealer dealt her a card face down. She sat there stiffly, as the dealer turned over his hole card. He had an 8 for a 17 and had to stand. He then turned over the double down card. It was a 6!

"See, I told you it's all luck," the lady said to me. "Gamble, gamble, gamble, Eddie boy, you so conservative. For a young man, so conservative."

"I'm not that young anymore."

"Oh, you young. Gray hairs disguise how young you are, Eddie boy. Young, young, young."

Well, what can you say to that?

SINGLE DECK SOFT TOTAL STRATEGY

The hands containing soft totals give the player the most trouble. The chart below should be memorized, and the best way to do that is to play out hands and refer to the chart till you have them down cold. It's easy to get mixed up with Soft totals. Most players don't really know what to do when they hold an Ace-3, for example. I've seen that hand and an Ace-2 doubled down against a dealer's 10 often enough to learn not to shake my head. I've seen more big bets lost by the inability of players to make correct decisions with soft hands.

So, it's essential that you learn correct Basic Strategy when playing out soft hands. To keep you on your toes we'll have a series of quizzes in the book. You should know every play without hesitation before you attempt to play for real money in a casino.

To refresh the reader's recollection, any hand that uses the Ace as an 11 forms a soft hand, and contains a soft total. To make this strategy table easier, we're combining all the possible plays.

SINGLE DECK SOFT TOTALS STRATEGY
Hitting - Standing - Doubling Down - Splitting

	2	3	4	5	6	7	8	9	10	A
AA	spl	spl	spl	spl	spl	spl	spl	spl	spl	spl
A2	H	H	D	D	D	H	H	H	H	H
A3	H	H	D	D	D	H	H	H	H	H
A4	H	H	D	D	D	H	H	H	H	H
A5	H	H	D	D	D	H	H	H	H	H
A6	D	D	D	D	D	H	H	H	H	H
A7	S	D	D	D	D	S	S	H	H	S
A8	S	S	S	S	D	S	S	S	S	S
A9	S	S	S	S	S	S	S	S	S	S

H = Hit   **S** = Stand   **D** = Double   **spl** = Split

SOFT 12: ACE-ACE

We've covered the Ace-Ace holding before. It's an ideal split, with each ace forming the base of an 11, ready to receive a 10 for that 21. Remember, a 21 after splitting formed by an ace and 10 is not a blackjack, just a 21, and so don't expect to be paid off at 3-2.

SOFT 13-16: A2-A5

The Ace-2, Ace-3, Ace-4 and Ace-5 (soft totals of 13-16) should either be hit or doubled down. One never stays with these weak totals. You can always improve them without worrying about busting. Against the dealer's worst upcards, the 4-6, you double them down. Against all other upcards, you hit them. Never, never stand with them!

SOFT 17: A6

The Ace-6 gives the average player a lot of trouble. It's a 17, and there are many players who stand on that total, though *the correct play is never to stand on soft 17*. You're either going to hit it or double down.

A few years ago, I was at a $25 table downtown, with three other players. And each of them, when dealt a soft 17, stood. They were not only betting quarter chips but $100 chips. And they didn't know the first thing about the game.

The soft 17 is strong enough to double down against a dealer's 2-6 upcard. You don't want to double down on any card higher than a 6, for you may get an odd card while the dealer may have a standing 17 or higher, and you've gotten yourself a double loss. The reason you don't stand on a soft 17 against a 7 or any higher card is that you can't bust the soft 17, and if the dealer shows an 8 or higher, your 17 is probably a loser already.

At least try to improve it. Even against the dealer's 7, you don't play for a push. It's a bad percentage play.

If you get an ace, 2, 3 or 4, on the soft 17, you've improved your hand. Even if you get the worst possible card, a 9, you now have hard 16, and a chance to improve again against a dealer's 7 or higher upcard.

SOFT 18: A7

Soft 18 (Ace-7) is another tough card holding for most players. They don't realize that a double down is a strong play against a dealer's 3-6, his magic stiff cards. It's a hand you stand with against the dealer's 2 or Ace, the two ends of the card spectrum, but you hit it against a dealer's 9 or

10. Why against the 9 or 10? If we assume the 10s are the most prevalent cards in the deck, there's a good chance the dealer is holding a 19 or 20, and our soft 18 loses to these holdings. We don't want to go down without a struggle.

One of the biggest bets I have ever made presented me with that situation. I was playing head-to-head with the dealer and had a humongous wager out. A floorman was watching. I had been losing and this one bet would put me ahead. I was dealt an Ace-7 and the dealer showed a 10.

I hesitated for a moment, but my mind told me—*make the right move, jerk*—and the right move is to hit the soft 17. I hit it and got a 4, for a hard 12. Now I definitely had to hit again and got an ace, for a hard 13. The cards were grinding me out emotionally. I hit again and got an 8! I couldn't believe it. The dealer turned over a 10 as his hole card for a 20, but I beat him. Call it luck, but I found that luck follows good play and bad luck follows in the heavy footsteps of foolish moves.

SOFT 19: A8

Ace-8 is a soft 19, a very strong hand, and you'd only double down this total against a dealer's 6, his worst up-card. Sometimes I've avoided this move, because it's an expert play and I was already drawing heat from the casino. If I had doubled down, I was sure I'd be barred. But it's the correct play.

SOFT 20: A9

Ace-9 is a soft 20, and you're satisfied with that total any day in the week. You don't tamper with this hand. Just stand on it.

THE SNAPPER: A10

And finally, Ace-10, the natural, *the snapper*, the best of all hands. Turn it over and collect your 3-2 payoff. Without hesitation.

8

MULTIPLE DECK BASIC STRATEGY

MULTIPLE DECK HITTING VS. STANDING

This table is good for Atlantic City, Las Vegas Strip and other games where four or six decks are used.

	2	3	4	5	6	7	8	9	10	A
MULTIPLE DECK HITTING VS. STANDING Hard Totals										
11/less	H	H	H	H	H	H	H	H	H	H
12	H	H	S	S	S	H	H	H	H	H
13	S	S	S	S	S	H	H	H	H	H
14	S	S	S	S	S	H	H	H	H	H
15	S	S	S	S	S	H	H	H	H	H
16	S	S	S	S	S	H	H	H	H	H
17-21	S	S	S	S	S	S	S	S	S	S

H = Hit   **S** = Stand

MULTIPLE DECK SPLITTING PAIRS

This table is for use in Atlantic City, Las Vegas and other locations, when playing in four or six deck games, without a surrender option, but where doubling down after splitting is permitted.

MULTIPLE DECK SPLITTING PAIRS
Doubling After Splitting

	2	3	4	5	6	7	8	9	10	A
22	spl	spl	spl	spl	spl	spl				
33	spl	spl	spl	spl	spl	spl				
44				spl	spl					
55										
66	spl	spl	spl	spl	spl					
77	spl	spl	spl	spl	spl	spl				
88	spl	spl	spl	spl	spl	spl	spl	spl	spl	spl
99	spl	spl	spl	spl	spl		spl	spl		
1010										
AA	spl	spl	spl	spl	spl	spl	spl	spl	spl	spl

spl = Split   **Blank** = Do Not Split

DOUBLING AFTER SPLITTING DIFFERENCES

Note the differences between playing in a multiple deck game in either Atlantic City or Las Vegas, where four or six decks are used and a player can double down after splitting, as against a single deck game in downtown Las Vegas, where one can't double down after splitting.

First of all, you split more aggressively where doubling down after splitting is permitted. Both the deuces and treys are split whenever the dealer shows a 2-7 as his or her upcard. Fours are split against a dealer's 5 or 6, whereas in a game without doubling down after splitting, the 4s wouldn't be split. It is with these smaller cards that most of the change is concentrated. Here's why.

In a game without doubling down after splitting, you don't want to split 2s against a dealer's 2, or 3s against a dealer's 2 or 3. There's no percentage in the play for you're risking doubling your money on weak small cards. But in Atlantic City or on the Strip, if you can double down after splitting, you may get a good card on a 2 or 3 that will allow you to double down.

Let's follow such a play. You hold 2s and the dealer shows a 2. You split them, putting out another bet equal to your original bet, and now you're playing each deuce as a separate hand. On the first deuce you get a 9 for an 11 and double down. You then get a 10 for a 21. On the second 2, you get an 8 for a 10 and double down against the dealer's 2. You get an 8 for an 18. The dealer turns over his hole card, which is a 10, for a hard 12. He hits and gets a 3 and has to hit his hard 15 again and gets a 10 and busts. By splitting the 2s, you've quadrupled your winnings.

It is this option, exercised at the right times, that can give you some nifty wins.

Many multiple deck games you will play will not allow you to double down after splitting pairs. We show that strategy below.

MULTIPLE DECK SPLITTING PAIRS
No Doubling Down After Splitting

	2	3	4	5	6	7	8	9	10	A
22			spl	spl	spl	spl				
33			spl	spl	spl	spl				
44										
55										
66		spl	spl	spl	spl					
77	spl	spl	spl	spl	spl	spl				
88	spl	spl	spl	spl	spl	spl	spl	spl	spl	spl
99	spl	spl	spl	spl	spl		spl	spl		
1010										
AA	spl	spl	spl	spl	spl	spl	spl	spl	spl	spl

spl = Split   **Blank** = Do Not Split

MULTIPLE DECK DOUBLING DOWN - HARD TOTALS

Note that the strategy for hard doubling down is much more conservative in four and six deck games. There are many more cards that can come up to hurt a double down, even though the decks have the same percentages of big cards. The ace is much more powerful in the dealer's hand in multiple deck games than it is in a single deck game and you must be aware of its strength.

MULTIPLE DECK DOUBLING DOWN
Hard Totals

	2	3	4	5	6	7	8	9	10	A
8										
9		D	D	D	D					
10	D	D	D	D	D	D	D	D		
11	D	D	D	D	D	D	D	D	D	

D = Double Down   **Blank** = Do Not Double Down

DOUBLING HARD 11 - MULTIPLE DECK

Even with an 11, our most powerful hand for doubling down, we don't double down against the dealer's ace.

DOUBLING HARD 10 - MULTIPLE DECK

With a 10, we double down against the 2-9, but not against the 10 or ace.

DOUBLING HARD 9 - MULTIPLE DECK

With a 9, we double down only against the stiff 3s, 4s, 5s and 6s, but not against the 2, as we do in a single deck game.

DOUBLING HARD 8 - MULTIPLE DECK

While we can double down with an 8 total in a single deck game, we don't dare do this in a multiple deck game where the 8 loses considerable strength as a base for doubling down.

MULTIPLE DECK SOFT TOTAL STRATEGY

MULTIPLE DECK SOFT TOTAL STRATEGY
Hitting • Standing • Doubling Down • Splitting

	2	3	4	5	6	7	8	9	10	A
AA	spl	spl	spl	spl	spl	spl	spl	spl	spl	spl
A2	H	H	H	D	D	H	H	H	H	H
A3	H	H	H	D	D	H	H	H	H	H
A4	H	H	D	D	D	H	H	H	H	H
A5	H	H	D	D	D	H	H	H	H	H
A6	H	D	D	D	D	H	H	H	H	H
A7	S	D	D	D	D	S	S	H	H	H
A8	S	S	S	S	S	S	S	S	S	S
A9	S	S	S	S	S	S	S	S	S	S

H = Hit   **S** = Stand   **D** = Double   **spl** = Split

SOFT 13-16

When playing in multiple deck games, soft doubling down is much more restrictive. The soft 13 and soft 14 hands can only be doubled down against a 5 or 6, and the soft 15 and soft 16 hands against a dealer's 4-6, the heart of his stiff cards.

SOFT 17 - MULTIPLE DECK

A soft 17, which in a single deck game can be doubled down against a 2-6 is now limited to 3-6, as is the soft 18.

SOFT 18 - MULTIPLE DECK

Because of the power of the dealer's ace in multiple deck games, the Ace-7 will be hit when the dealer has an ace as his upcard, whereas in the single deck game, the player stands on his soft 18 against the ace.

SOFT 19-20 MULTIPLE DECK

The Ace-8 and Ace-9 are standing hands in multiple deck games, whereas in a single deck game, a really skillful play is to double down with the soft 19 against a dealer's 6.

NORTHERN NEVADA BASIC STRATEGY

Be aware of the following variations.

Doubling down on 10 and 11 is permitted, with no other double downs allowed. Therefore, all soft totals should be hit and played according to the soft total chart. An example would be this:

You're dealt an Ace-6 and the dealer shows a 4. Since the correct play is to double down, and this isn't allowed, hit the soft 17. If it turns into a hard total of 12 or more, then stand. A little practice will enable you to work out all the strategies.

One other variation. If you are dealt any kind of soft 18, such as Ace-7 or Ace-2-5, hit it against the dealer's Ace.

MULTIPLE DECK DOUBLING DOWN
Northern Nevada - Doubling on 10 and 11 Only

	2	3	4	5	6	7	8	9	10	A
10	D	D	D	D	D	D	D	D		
11	D	D	D	D	D	D	D	D	D	

D = Double Down　　　**Blank** = Hit, Do Not Double Down

MULTIPLE DECK EARLY SURRENDER

Early surrender, the option to divest yourself of half your bet and your hand before the dealer peeks to see if he or she has a blackjack, was once standard in Atlantic City, but today, it's difficult to find such a game. If you do, however, here is what you surrender:

Against the Dealer's Ace:
Surrender the hard total of 5, 6 and 7. Also hard totals of 12-17.

Against the Dealer's 10:
Surrender all hard 14s, 15s and 16s, including 7-7 & 8-8.

Against the Dealer's 9:
Surrender a hard 16, but split 8-8.

MULTIPLE DECK WITH EARLY SURRENDER

	2	3	4	5	6	7	8	9	10	A
5										X
6										X
7										X
12										X
13										X
14									X	X
15									X	X
16								X	X	X
17										X
77									X	
88								*	X	

X = Surrender   **Blank** = Do Not Surrender

*Do not surrender 88 vs. 9 - split

MULTIPLE DECK WITH CONVENTIONAL (LATE) SURRENDER

Conventional surrender allows you to give up one-half of your bet and your playing hand only after the dealer has checked to see if he or she has a blackjack.

Against the Dealer's Ace:
Surrender hard 16 (but split the 8-8)

Against the Dealer's 10:
Surrender 15s and 16s (but split 8-8)

Against the Dealer's 9:
Surrender hard 16s (but split 8-8)

	2	3	4	5	6	7	8	9	10	A
MULTIPLE DECK WITH CONVENTIONAL (LATE) SURRENDER										
15								X		
16								X	X	X
88								X**		

X = Surrender   **Blank** = Do Not Surrender

*Do not surrender 88 vs. 10 - split

9

THE MASTER CHARTS

THE IMPORTANCE OF BASIC STRATEGY

Basic Strategy is the foundation of winning blackjack. You must master it before you think of playing for actual cash in a casino. You should learn all the correct strategies for every type of game, and particularly, those strategies that apply to the game you're about to play.

For example, if you're heading for Vegas, there's no need to study the Northern Nevada strategies. If your intention is to play single deck blackjack in Vegas, then concentrate on that, rather than the multiple deck game.

When playing in any particular jurisdiction, always look for the best game. All other things being equal, a single deck game is the best, followed by the double deck game, followed by four and then six decks. Sometimes, as in Atlantic City or the riverboats, you'll find no single deck games. So try to find a four deck, rather than a six deck game.

In Vegas, where multiple deck as well as single deck games abound, play the game you feel most comfortable at. It will probably be single deck. As you study counting, you'll find that the single deck game is the easiest to master and to play at. That's because, with only 52 cards, the decks are shuffled more often, and you start fresh, with a zero count.

In multiple deck games, the count goes on and on, and with the pressure of play and the distractions in any casino, you may lose the count or have your mind drift away to other thoughts. That happens, and it happens more often the more tired you get. That's natural, and don't fight it. If you can't even remember what basic strategy calls for in certain situations, then stop playing, cash in and take a break.

However, multiple deck games can give you long wins of favorability in which you can raise your bets continually, the dealer will not usually be able to shuffle up. Therefore, when playing in a jurisdiction, such as Atlantic City or on the riverboats where only multiple decks are used, practice patience and wait for that favorable run of cards.

A final note: Study the tables for the games you're going to play, and practice with a deck or a number of decks of cards. Deal yourself hands for hours at an end, till you know every play by heart. That's your goal—to know it 100%. Anything less will put you at a disadvantage to the casino.

With correct basic strategy, you're even, and with card counting and altering of bets, you'll have a solid advantage over the casino.

Note: Riverboat and Indian Reservation Blackjack

The Basic Strategies for these areas can vary greatly due to the wide variance of states you may find blackjack. However, wherever you may find blackjack, the rules for these games will approximate those for Las Vegas or Atlantic City, if not be exactly the same, and thus the Master Strategy Charts will be perfectly valid for these games.

THE MASTER CHARTS

The following Master Charts summarize the Basic Strategies.

MULTIPLE DECK MASTER CHART
Las Vegas
(Typical Riverboat & Indian Casino Rules)

<u>No</u> Doubling Allowed After Splitting - <u>No</u> Surrender

These represent typical rules at these locales, but as discussed previously, many variations can be found. Thus, if doubling after splitting is allowed, use the Atlantic City Master Chart—the main difference in that chart reflecting that very rule—doubling after splitting.

THE MASTER CHARTS

MULTIPLE DECK MASTER CHART
Las Vegas, Riverboat, Indian Casino
(No Doubling Allowed After Splitting - No Surrender Allowed)

	2	3	4	5	6	7	8	9	10	A
7/less	H	H	H	H	H	H	H	H	H	H
8	H	H	H	H	H	H	H	H	H	H
9	H	D	D	D	D	H	H	H	H	H
10	D	D	D	D	D	D	D	D	H	H
11	D	D	D	D	D	D	D	D	D	H
12	H	H	S	S	S	H	H	H	H	H
13	S	S	S	S	S	H	H	H	H	H
14	S	S	S	S	S	H	H	H	H	H
15	S	S	S	S	S	H	H	H	H	H
16	S	S	S	S	S	H	H	H	H	H
A2	H	H	H	D	D	H	H	H	H	H
A3	H	H	H	D	D	H	H	H	H	H
A4	H	H	D	D	D	H	H	H	H	H
A5	H	H	D	D	D	H	H	H	H	H
A6	H	D	D	D	D	H	H	H	H	H
A7	S	D	D	D	D	S	S	H	H	H
A8	S	S	S	S	S	S	S	S	S	S
A9	S	S	S	S	S	S	S	S	S	S
22	H	H	spl	spl	spl	spl	H	H	H	H
33	H	H	spl	spl	spl	spl	H	H	H	H
66	H	spl	spl	spl	spl	H	H	H	H	H
77	spl	spl	spl	spl	spl	spl	H	H	H	H
88	spl	spl	spl	spl	spl	spl	spl	spl	spl	spl
99	spl	spl	spl	spl	spl	S	spl	spl	S	S
AA	spl	spl	spl	spl	spl	spl	spl	spl	spl	spl

H = Hit **S** = Stand **D** = Double **spl** = Split
Do not split 44, 55 (double on 55) and 10s. Always split 88 and AA

MULTIPLE DECK MASTER CHART
Las Vegas
(Typical Riverboat & Indian Casino Rules)

No Doubling After Splitting - Late Surrender Allowed

Use this chart when surrender is allowed in a multiple deck game, but not doubling after splitting.

MULTIPLE DECK MASTER CHART
Las Vegas, Riverboat, Indian Casino

(No Doubling Allowed After Splitting - Late Surrender Allowed)

	2	3	4	5	6	7	8	9	10	A
7/less	H	H	H	H	H	H	H	H	H	H
8	H	H	H	H	H	H	H	H	H	H
9	H	D	D	D	D	H	H	H	H	H
10	D	D	D	D	D	D	D	D	H	H
11	D	D	D	D	D	D	D	D	D	H
12	H	H	S	S	S	H	H	H	H	H
13	S	S	S	S	S	H	H	H	H	H
14	S	S	S	S	S	H	H	H	H	H
15	S	S	S	S	S	H	H	H	X	H
16	S	S	S	S	S	H	H	X	X	X
A2	H	H	H	D	D	H	H	H	H	H
A3	H	H	H	D	D	H	H	H	H	H
A4	H	H	D	D	D	H	H	H	H	H
A5	H	H	D	D	D	H	H	H	H	H
A6	H	D	D	D	D	H	H	H	H	H
A7	S	D	D	D	D	S	S	H	H	H
A8	S	S	S	S	S	S	S	S	S	S
A9	S	S	S	S	S	S	S	S	S	S
22	H	H	spl	spl	spl	spl	H	H	H	H
33	H	H	spl	spl	spl	spl	H	H	H	H
66	H	spl	spl	spl	spl	H	H	H	H	H
77	spl	spl	spl	spl	spl	spl	H	H	H	H
88	spl	spl	spl	spl	spl	spl	spl	spl	spl	spl
99	spl	spl	spl	spl	spl	S	spl	spl	S	S
AA	spl	spl	spl	spl	spl	spl	spl	spl	spl	spl

H = Hit **S** = Stand **D** = Double **spl** = Split **X** = Surrender
Do not split 44, 55 (double on 55) and 10s. Always split 88 and AA

MULTIPLE DECK MASTER CHART
Favorable Multiple Deck Rules

Doubling Allowed After Splitting - Surrender Allowed

This Master Chart represents the correct Basic Strategy for multiple deck games when both these favorable rules are found together.

MULTIPLE DECK MASTER CHART
Favorable Multiple Deck Rules
(Doubling Allowed After Splitting - Late Surrender Allowed)

	2	3	4	5	6	7	8	9	10	A
7/less	H	H	H	H	H	H	H	H	H	H
8	H	H	H	H	H	H	H	H	H	H
9	H	D	D	D	D	H	H	H	H	H
10	D	D	D	D	D	D	D	D	H	H
11	D	D	D	D	D	D	D	D	D	H
12	H	H	S	S	S	H	H	H	H	H
13	S	S	S	S	S	H	H	H	H	H
14	S	S	S	S	S	H	H	H	H	H
15	S	S	S	S	S	H	H	H	X	H
16	S	S	S	S	S	H	H	X	X	X
A2	H	H	H	D	D	H	H	H	H	H
A3	H	H	H	D	D	H	H	H	H	H
A4	H	H	D	D	D	H	H	H	H	H
A5	H	H	D	D	D	H	H	H	H	H
A6	H	D	D	D	D	H	H	H	H	H
A7	S	D	D	D	D	S	S	H	H	H
A8	S	S	S	S	S	S	S	S	S	S
A9	S	S	S	S	S	S	S	S	S	S
22	spl	spl	spl	spl	spl	spl	H	H	H	H
33	spl	spl	spl	spl	spl	spl	H	H	H	H
44	H	H	H	spl	spl	H	H	H	H	H
66	spl	spl	spl	spl	spl	H	H	H	H	H
77	spl	spl	spl	spl	spl	spl	H	H	H	H
88	spl	spl	spl	spl	spl	spl	spl	spl	spl	spl
99	spl	spl	spl	spl	spl	S	spl	spl	S	S
AA	spl	spl	spl	spl	spl	spl	spl	spl	spl	spl

H = Hit   **S** = Stand   **D** = Double   **spl** = Split   **X** = Surrender
Do not split 55 and 10s. Always split 88 and AA

MULTIPLE DECK MASTER CHART
Northern Nevada

No Doubling Allowed After Splitting - No Surrender

The player is restricted to doubling down on totals of 10 and 11 only.

MULTIPLE DECK MASTER CHART
Northern Nevada

(No Doubling Allowed After Splitting - No Surrender)

	2	3	4	5	6	7	8	9	10	A
7/less	H	H	H	H	H	H	H	H	H	H
8	H	H	H	H	H	H	H	H	H	H
9	H	H	H	H	H	H	H	H	H	H
10	D	D	D	D	D	D	D	D	H	H
11	D	D	D	D	D	D	D	D	D	H
12	H	H	S	S	S	H	H	H	H	H
13	S	S	S	S	S	H	H	H	H	H
14	S	S	S	S	S	H	H	H	H	H
15	S	S	S	S	S	H	H	H	H	H
16	S	S	S	S	S	H	H	H	H	H
A2	H	H	H	H	H	H	H	H	H	H
A3	H	H	H	H	H	H	H	H	H	H
A4	H	H	H	H	H	H	H	H	H	H
A5	H	H	H	H	H	H	H	H	H	H
A6	H	H	H	H	H	H	H	H	H	H
A7	S	S	S	S	S	S	S	H	H	H
A8	S	S	S	S	S	S	S	S	S	S
A9	S	S	S	S	S	S	S	S	S	S
22	H	H	spl	spl	spl	spl	H	H	H	H
33	H	H	spl	spl	spl	spl	H	H	H	H
66	H	spl	spl	spl	spl	H	H	H	H	H
77	spl	spl	spl	spl	spl	spl	H	H	H	H
88	spl	spl	spl	spl	spl	spl	spl	spl	spl	spl
99	spl	spl	spl	spl	spl	S	spl	spl	S	S
AA	spl	spl	spl	spl	spl	spl	spl	spl	spl	spl

H = Hit   **S** = Stand   **D** = Double   **spl** = Split

Do not split 44, 55 (double on 55) and 10s. Always split 88 and AA

MULTIPLE DECK MASTER CHART
Atlantic City

Doubling Allowed After Splitting - No Surrender

If you find a Las Vegas, riverboat or Indian casino multiple deck game with the doubling after splitting option, than this Master Chart is applicable.

MULTIPLE DECK MASTER CHART
Atlantic City

Doubling Allowed After Splitting - No Surrender

	2	3	4	5	6	7	8	9	10	A
7/less	H	H	H	H	H	H	H	H	H	H
8	H	H	H	H	H	H	H	H	H	H
9	H	D	D	D	D	H	H	H	H	H
10	D	D	D	D	D	D	D	D	H	H
11	D	D	D	D	D	D	D	D	D	H
12	H	H	S	S	S	H	H	H	H	H
13	S	S	S	S	S	H	H	H	H	H
14	S	S	S	S	S	H	H	H	H	H
15	S	S	S	S	S	H	H	H	H	H
16	S	S	S	S	S	H	H	H	H	H
A2	H	H	H	D	D	H	H	H	H	H
A3	H	H	H	D	D	H	H	H	H	H
A4	H	H	D	D	D	H	H	H	H	H
A5	H	H	D	D	D	H	H	H	H	H
A6	H	D	D	D	D	H	H	H	H	H
A7	S	D	D	D	D	S	S	H	H	H
A8	S	S	S	S	S	S	S	S	S	S
A9	S	S	S	S	S	S	S	S	S	S
22	spl	spl	spl	spl	spl	spl	H	H	H	H
33	spl	spl	spl	spl	spl	spl	H	H	H	H
44	H	H	H	spl	spl	H	H	H	H	H
66	spl	spl	spl	spl	spl	H	H	H	H	H
77	spl	spl	spl	spl	spl	spl	H	H	H	H
88	spl	spl	spl	spl	spl	spl	spl	spl	spl	spl
99	spl	spl	spl	spl	spl	S	spl	spl	S	S
AA	spl	spl	spl	spl	spl	spl	spl	spl	spl	spl

H = Hit   **S** = Stand   **D** = Double   **spl** = Split

Do not split 55 and 10s. Always split 88 and AA

MULTIPLE DECK MASTER CHART
European No Hole Card Style

<u>No</u> Doubling After Splitting - <u>No</u> Surrender Allowed

European style rules which can be found not only in Europe, but in many locales around the world, restrict the player to doubling on 9-11 only and employ the no hole card rule—a disadvantageous rule whereby the dealer doesn't check his hole card for a blackjack until *after* the players have acted on their hands. Thus, the extra bets on doubled or split hands will be lost if the dealer makes a blackjack, as opposed to U.S. casinos where the extra bets will be returned.

MULTIPLE DECK MASTER CHART
European No Hole Card Style

No Doubling Allowed After Splitting - No Surrender Allowed

	2	3	4	5	6	7	8	9	10	A
7/less	H	H	H	H	H	H	H	H	H	H
8	H	H	H	H	H	H	H	H	H	H
9	H	D	D	D	D	H	H	H	H	H
10	D	D	D	D	D	D	D	D	H	H
11	D	D	D	D	D	D	D	D	H	H
12	H	H	S	S	S	H	H	H	H	H
13	S	S	S	S	S	H	H	H	H	H
14	S	S	S	S	S	H	H	H	H	H
15	S	S	S	S	S	H	H	H	H	H
16	S	S	S	S	S	H	H	H	H	H
A2	H	H	H	H	H	H	H	H	H	H
A3	H	H	H	H	H	H	H	H	H	H
A4	H	H	H	H	H	H	H	H	H	H
A5	H	H	H	H	H	H	H	H	H	H
A6	H	H	H	H	H	H	H	H	H	H
A7	S	S	S	S	S	S	S	H	H	H
A8	S	S	S	S	S	S	S	S	S	S
A9	S	S	S	S	S	S	S	S	S	S
22	H	H	spl	spl	spl	spl	H	H	H	H
33	H	H	spl	spl	spl	spl	H	H	H	H
66	H	spl	spl	spl	spl	H	H	H	H	H
77	spl	spl	spl	spl	spl	spl	H	H	H	H
88	spl	spl	spl	spl	spl	spl	spl	spl	H	H
99	spl	spl	spl	spl	spl	S	spl	spl	S	S
AA	spl	spl	spl	spl	spl	spl	spl	spl	spl	H

H = Hit   **S** = Stand   **D** = Double   **spl** = Split

Do not split 44, 55 and 10s

SINGLE DECK MASTER CHART
Northern Nevada

<u>No</u> Doubling Allowed After Splitting - <u>No</u> Surrender

The player is restricted to doubling down on totals of 10 and 11 only.

SINGLE DECK MASTER CHART
Northern Nevada

(No Doubling Allowed After Splitting - No Surrender)

	2	3	4	5	6	7	8	9	10	A
7/less	H	H	H	H	H	H	H	H	H	H
8	H	H	H	H	H	H	H	H	H	H
9	H	H	H	H	H	H	H	H	H	H
10	D	D	D	D	D	D	D	D	H	H
11	D	D	D	D	D	D	D	D	D	D
12	H	H	S	S	S	H	H	H	H	H
13	S	S	S	S	S	H	H	H	H	H
14	S	S	S	S	S	H	H	H	H	H
15	S	S	S	S	S	H	H	H	H	H
16	S	S	S	S	S	H	H	H	H	H
A2	H	H	H	H	H	H	H	H	H	H
A3	H	H	H	H	H	H	H	H	H	H
A4	H	H	H	H	H	H	H	H	H	H
A5	H	H	H	H	H	H	H	H	H	H
A6	H	H	H	H	H	H	H	H	H	H
A7	S	S	S	S	S	S	S	H	H	S
A8	S	S	S	S	S	S	S	S	S	S
A9	S	S	S	S	S	S	S	S	S	S
22	H	spl	spl	spl	spl	spl	H	H	H	H
33	H	H	spl	spl	spl	spl	H	H	H	H
66	spl	spl	spl	spl	spl	H	H	H	H	H
77	spl	spl	spl	spl	spl	spl	H	H	S	H
88	spl	spl	spl	spl	spl	spl	spl	spl	spl	spl
99	spl	spl	spl	spl	spl	S	spl	spl	S	S
AA	spl	spl	spl	spl	spl	spl	spl	spl	spl	spl

H = Hit   **S** = Stand   **D** = Double   **spl** = Split

Do not split 44, 55 (double on 55) and 10s. Always split 88 and AA

SINGLE DECK MASTER CHART
Las Vegas • Single Deck

Doubling Allowed After Splitting - No Surrender

Notice the more aggressive pair splitting due to the doubling after splitting rule. This is even more aggressive than the multiple deck games that allow doubling after splitting.

SINGLE DECK MASTER CHART
Las Vegas
(Doubling Allowed After Splitting - No Surrender)

	2	3	4	5	6	7	8	9	10	A
7/less	H	H	H	H	H	H	H	H	H	H
62	H	H	H	H	H	H	H	H	H	H
44/53	H	H	H	D	D	H	H	H	H	H
9	D	D	D	D	D	H	H	H	H	H
10	D	D	D	D	D	D	D	D	H	H
11	D	D	D	D	D	D	D	D	D	D
12	H	H	S	S	S	H	H	H	H	H
13	S	S	S	S	S	H	H	H	H	H
14	S	S	S	S	S	H	H	H	H	H
15	S	S	S	S	S	H	H	H	H	H
16	S	S	S	S	S	H	H	H	H	H
A2	H	H	D	D	D	H	H	H	H	H
A3	H	H	D	D	D	H	H	H	H	H
A4	H	H	D	D	D	H	H	H	H	H
A5	H	H	D	D	D	H	H	H	H	H
A6	D	D	D	D	D	H	H	H	H	H
A7	S	D	D	D	D	S	S	H	H	S
A8	S	S	S	S	D	S	S	S	S	S
A9	S	S	S	S	S	S	S	S	S	S
22	spl	spl	spl	spl	spl	spl	H	H	H	H
33	spl	spl	spl	spl	spl	spl	H	H	H	H
44	H	H	spl	spl	spl	H	H	H	H	H
66	spl	spl	spl	spl	spl	spl	H	H	H	H
77	spl	spl	spl	spl	spl	spl	spl	H	S	H
88	spl	spl	spl	spl	spl	spl	spl	spl	spl	spl
99	spl	spl	spl	spl	spl	S	spl	spl	S	S
AA	spl	spl	spl	spl	spl	spl	spl	spl	spl	spl

H = Hit   **S** = Stand   **D** = Double   **spl** = Split
Do not split 55 (double on 55) and 10s. Always split 88 and AA

SINGLE DECK MASTER CHART
Las Vegas • Single Deck

No Doubling Allowed After Splitting - No Surrender

SINGLE DECK MASTER CHART
Las Vegas

(No Doubling Allowed After Splitting - No Surrender)

	2	3	4	5	6	7	8	9	10	A
7/less	H	H	H	H	H	H	H	H	H	H
62	H	H	H	H	H	H	H	H	H	H
44/53	H	H	H	D	D	H	H	H	H	H
9	D	D	D	D	D	H	H	H	H	H
10	D	D	D	D	D	D	D	D	H	H
11	D	D	D	D	D	D	D	D	D	D
12	H	H	S	S	S	H	H	H	H	H
13	S	S	S	S	S	H	H	H	H	H
14	S	S	S	S	S	H	H	H	H	H
15	S	S	S	S	S	H	H	H	H	H
16	S	S	S	S	S	H	H	H	H	H
A2	H	H	D	D	D	H	H	H	H	H
A3	H	H	D	D	D	H	H	H	H	H
A4	H	H	D	D	D	H	H	H	H	H
A5	H	H	D	D	D	H	H	H	H	H
A6	D	D	D	D	D	H	H	H	H	H
A7	S	D	D	D	D	S	S	H	H	S
A8	S	S	S	S	D	S	S	S	S	S
A9	S	S	S	S	S	S	S	S	S	S
22	H	spl	spl	spl	spl	spl	H	H	H	H
33	H	H	spl	spl	spl	spl	H	H	H	H
66	spl	spl	spl	spl	spl	H	H	H	H	H
77	spl	spl	spl	spl	spl	spl	H	H	S	H
88	spl	spl	spl	spl	spl	spl	spl	spl	spl	spl
99	spl	spl	spl	spl	spl	S	spl	spl	S	S
AA	spl	spl	spl	spl	spl	spl	spl	spl	spl	spl

H = Hit   **S** = Stand   **D** = Double   **spl** = Split

Do not split 44, 55 (double on 55) and 10s. Always split 88 and AA

10

CARD COUNTING

INTRODUCTION

Most beginners when they hear the term **card counting**, imagine that they're going to be involved in a tedious and complicated method of keeping track of the cards as they're played out. But nothing could be further from the truth. Our card-counting method is simplicity itself, and beyond simplicity, it's very effective. It's a winner!

We don't expect you to memorize all the cards that are dealt out. Nor do we ask you to keep track of all the cards that remain in play. What you're going to learn is a simple + and - count. This count deals with only a limited number of key cards. You balance one set of unfavorable cards against another set of favorable cards. Then you come up with a number.

If the number is +, then the deck or decks are favorable to you. If the number is -, then the deck or decks are unfavorable. That's all there is to it.

Counting cards enables you to have an edge over the casino because of another important factor. Since you can alter your bets before each play, you're going to raise your bets when the deck or decks are favorable and lower your bets when they're unfavorable.

This gives you a solid advantage over the house. There will be times when the deck is super-favorable to you, and you'll have a maximum bet out. At other times, the deck will be neutral, and so you'll have your neutral bet out. Other times, the deck or decks will be unfavorable, and so you'll have your minimum bet out. We'll cover the size of the bets in another section. It's not always possible to put out a huge bet when the deck is super-favorable. This might cause casino **heat**, resulting in countermeasures or even barring.

What we'll show you is a good method of betting when you play, one that will win you money but keep you in action.

Let's now examine card counting. Years ago, I wrote about this method, referring to it as the Silberstang Method. It has other names, and other authors have modified it, but it's still a solid method of winning. It's a balancing method of counting, with a final + or - after each round of play. Or a neutral result.

THE COUNTING METHOD

This method will keep you in play without overwhelming you with complications and fatigue. It's very effective as well, a good combination.

Remember, there are thirteen cards in each suit, from the 2 to the ace. However four of these cards, the 10, jack, queen and king, all have the same 10-value. So, in essence, there are really ten different valued cards in the deck. Four of them are 10s. The 10s, together with the aces, are the cards the player wants to see remaining in the deck.

Here's the reason. The 10s form one base of blackjacks, the aces form the other base. Thus a 10-Ace pays you 3-2. If the dealer gets a blackjack, he only wins the bet; he doesn't collect 3-2. Also, the dealer is bound by certain rules of play. He must hit all 16s and stand on 17s, (unless he hits soft 17s). These are universal rules.

Since 10s predominate, we can get a good idea of the dealer's hole card. It is more likely to be a 10 than any other card. That is how we make our basic strategy considerations.

Let's assume we're playing single-deck blackjack, and it's just us head-to-head with the dealer. No one else is at the table. The dealer deals us Ace-Ace and shows an Ace. He asks if we want insurance. We shake our head "no." He peeks and doesn't have a 10 underneath. So it's our play.

We split the aces according to basic strategy, and get a 10 on each. We have two 21s. We can't lose. The dealer turns over his hole card, and has a pair of aces now: Ace-Ace. He hits and gets a 9 for his 21. It's a push.

To the average player, the dealer got himself a lucky card, and he plays on willy-nilly. But to the astute card-counter, what has happened is devastating. All four aces as well as two 10s have been removed from the

The 10s, together with the aces, are the cards you want to see remaining in the deck.

deck, and the player has nothing to show for it. From now on the deck is going to be unfavorable.

Why? Well, even if you don't know anything about counting cards, you realize that you're not going to be able to get a blackjack till the cards are reshuffled. There are no more aces.

The lack of aces will also hurt us because we won't have any soft totals that will enable us to use the doubling down option.

If we are dealt an Ace-5, for example, and the dealer shows a 6, it's a very favorable double down for us. But if we have a 4-2 and the dealer shows a 6, all we can do is hit the hand.

The fact that two 10s have also been removed from play hurts us as well. The dealer is bound by strict rules of play and with many cards in the deck, he can make his stiff hands of 12, 13, 14, 15 and 16. But we're stuck. Suppose we have a 10-6 and the dealer shows a 5. We can't hit that hand. But if the dealer turns over his hole card and has an 8-5 and hits it with a 4, he has a 17 and beats us.

Card counting is worthwhile if we just remember the above hand where all four aces came out. That's an unusual round of play, but it serves our purpose in showing that what has been dealt out is important in determining what will happen in the future in blackjack.

In multiple deck blackjack removal of four aces is not as dramatic but it still has a negative effect.

And now to our count:

The Count

- We give each 10 a value of **- 1**
- We give each 3, 4, 5, 6 a value of **+1**
- We give the 2, 7, 8 and 9 a value of **0**
- We count aces separately

The reason we give the 10s a -1 is that each 10 dealt out of the deck, makes it weaker for the player, or more unfavorable. And conversely, each small card dealt out of the deck, makes it stronger for the player.

So, if we have a minus count, we know the deck is unfavorable. If we have a positive count, we know the deck is favorable, for the worst cards for the player, the 3, 4, 5 and 6 have been removed.

Now, here's how we balance the favorable and unfavorable cards.

Let's go back to our horror hand, where the player held Ace-10 and the dealer held Ace-Ace-9. Looking at our values, we have two 10s out for a count of -2. The 9 is neutral. We still have -2. All four aces are out. With the aces out, we have a super-negative situation, since we can no longer count on one of our key options, getting paid 3-2 for a blackjack. We can't get a blackjack now.

So we have a -2 with no aces. The deck is very negative.

PRACTICING THE COUNT

Let's now start fresh. The cards are reshuffled, two other players enter the game and sit next to us, on either side, and the dealer begins to deal. We are dealt a 10-5 and the dealer shows a 4 as his upcard. We start the count now on what we can see. One 10 = -1, but the 4 and 5 is +2. So far, the deck is +1. By balancing values we only have to keep one number in mind, the ratio of unfavorable cards to favorable ones, with the aces separately counted.

The first player turns over an 8-3 to double down against the dealer. The 8 is neutral, but the 3 makes the deck +2. His card is dealt face down, but he shakes his head looking at it, for it's a 2. Another neutral card. The last player now acts. We, of course, have stood on our miserable total of 15. He hesitates, then decides not to hit his hand.

The dealer turns over an 8 as his hole card. A neutral card. He hits his hand and gets a 10 and busts. The deck is now +1. He turns over the last player's cards. He held a 6-6. The deck is now +3. The last player should have split his 6s, but didn't. No matter. With a +3 deck, and no aces out, the deck is super-favorable. We are paid off, and leave our doubled bet on the table.

On the next hand we get 10-10. Beautiful. The dealer turns over a 9 as his upcard. The first player turns over a blackjack. The two 10s bring the deck down to +1, still favorable, with one ace played out. The last player hesitates again, then stands. He has a 9-6.

We balance them and the deck is now +2. The dealer turns over a 10 as his hole card and now the deck is +1. One ace played out. So far 19 cards have been played out.

We don't have to keep track of how many cards have been played. We can assume that 2 1/2 cards per participant per round are played. Or 3, to make it easier. If you're head-to-head with the dealer, about five cards a round are played. If the cards are standing hands, then less will be dealt out. So here, in a four-handed game, including the dealer, ten cards per round is the norm.

Two aces should theoretically have been played out. Since only one has been played, the deck is slightly favorable at +1, and slightly more ace-rich.

It's still worth a bigger bet. A new round of cards are now dealt out, and we keep track in the same manner, as we see cards, rather than scanning the table at the end of play. It's easier to do our way, and also gives us the look of not really concentrating on what is happening, the sure sign of a card counter as far as casino personnel are concerned.

Let's now run through another round of cards. We'll just list the cards and show the count as it goes on.

First Round of Play	
(three players and a dealer)	
• 10-3-4	+1
• 10-10	- 1
• 8-9	- 1
• 10-6-6	0

We followed the cards as they were dealt, keeping the count going hand by hand. In the first hand, the 3-4 gave

124

us +2, and the 10 made it +1. The two 10s in the second hand reduced the count to -1. The 8-9 in the third hand are both neutral cards. The dealer showed a 10 as his upcard, hit his hard 16 and busted with another 6, but that made the count even again, since the two 6s were +2 and the 10 a -1.

Anytime the cards are reshuffled by the dealer, we begin the count as zero.

COUNTING UNSEEN CARDS

Should we be fortunate in seeing the dealer's burn card, we start our count off with this card. For example, suppose you're playing in a casino where the dealer places the **burn card** (the card off the top of the deck) under the deck he's holding. And suppose he's sloppy about that move, and we see the burn card. Let's say it's a 10. Our count begins at -1. If it's a 4, our count begins at +1. Any card we see we count.

There may be times when we don't see players' cards during any round of play.

Sometimes, when a player busts, he puts all the cards together and turns them over so that we can't see all the cards. We have to make an educated guess. The cards are dealt face down for the most part in single deck games and that's a slight hindrance to our count.

Suppose the first baseman busts and the dealer snatches them away before we can see them all. The player had to hit, and did, taking one card, a 7. We also see his 10 but not the third card. We can assume the card was a 5 or 6, because what else could he have held that a 7 would bust? So, we know the count is even as far as that player is concerned.

That one was easy, but sometimes we just won't see the cards. We may be putting out a double down while the player is busting to our right and we miss his cards. It would be nice if we could say to the dealer, "Excuse me, I'm a card counter, so would you spread that fool's cards so I can keep the count going?" But that won't do. We make an educated guess on the unseen cards or we disregard them. There's nothing else we can do.

We won't always be able to see all the cards to get a completely accurate count at times. In those instances, we guess as closely as possible, rather than just giving up the count. The close guess is a better move for us rather than rubbing our minds blank because we missed a card or two.

In a multiple deck game, we see all the cards face up, so if we're alert, there's no reason to miss the correct count, whether or not a player busts.

In the next example, we're going to be at a table with three other players, and we're going to show the cards as they're dealt. Figure out the count after each round of play.

PRACTICE EXAMPLE #1

Your cards: 10-8

Dealer shows a 9. First baseman hits and gets a 5, then stands. Second baseman turns over a blackjack. Third player hits and gets a 2, hits again and gets a 6, then turns over a 10-4 after busting. Dealer's hole card is a 10. Dealer turns over first baseman's cards—he held a 7-6.

What's the count after this round of play?

The count is even, or zero. Here's how it's figured.

Your cards held a 10; that makes it -1 (8 is neutral). The dealer's 9 is neutral. First baseman's hit of a 5 is a +1, making the count even. Second basemen's blackjack contains a 10, making the count -1. Also important, one ace is played out. Third player has a 4, 6 and 10, bringing the count back to even. (2 is neutral). Dealer's hole card is a 10. Counting goes to -1. First baseman's unseen cards contain a 5, making the count even again. (7 is neutral).

As you can see, balancing cards for a count in this way, with a + or - result is simplicity itself. All it takes is practice, and we advise that you practice, because once you master card counting, the casino is going to bleed dollars to you.

Let's continue into the second round of play. Again, we'll show the cards, but you determine the count at the end of play.

PRACTICE EXAMPLE #2

You're dealt a 10-4

Dealer shows an 8. First baseman stands pat. Second baseman hits and gets a 3, hesitates, hits again and gets a 2, stands.

You hit and get a 10 and bust. Third player stands pat. Dealer turns over another 8 as his hole card, places the 8-8 carefully side by side and hits, getting a 10, and busts. He picks up chips and starts to pay off the players. The first baseman's cards are turned over. He held a 10-9. The second baseman's hole cards are an Ace-3. The third player held a 10-6.

What's the count?

The count is -1. Your 10-4 canceled each other out for an even count. Dealer's 8 is neutral. Still even. Second baseman's 3 made the count +1, with the 2 a neutral card. You're 10 hit brought the count back to even. Dealer's other 8 is neutral, but the 10 makes the count -1. First baseman's 10 makes it -2, with the 9 neutral. The second baseman's 3 made the count -1. The ace is now the second ace played out. The third player's 10-6 canceled themselves and the count stayed at -1.

If a third round of cards were dealt, you would start the count at -1. The count is always started where it left off the previous round. At the outset of play, before any cards are dealt for the first round, the count starts at even, or 0, in a single deck game.

All in all, thirteen cards were dealt out on the first round of play, and 13 more on the second round of play, for a total of 26 cards, just half the deck. As we mentioned, a quick formula we can use to know the number of cards dealt out is to give each participant, including the dealer, an average of 2.5 cards per round. With five participants (four players and the dealer) that would come to 12.5 cards or 13 cards to approximate—very close to what was actually dealt.

We mention this, because the count becomes more powerful the more the deck is penetrated. It is this *penetration* that allows us to make some pretty coups with card counting. Which leads us to the next aspect of the count, altering bets according to the count.

THE TRUE COUNT

What we have studied previously in counting cards is known as the **running count**. That is, the count reflects accurately the balance of 10s to other cards, 3-4 5-6, as they are dealt out. The count is shown either by a 0 (perfect balance); + (balance in favor of the player); or - (balance in favor of the dealer).

However, to get a more accurate idea of how good or bad the deck is to you, you want to know the true count.

The **true count** is determined by dividing the running count by the number of *half-decks* remaining to be dealt. This is a fairly universal method used by professional card counters. Instead of dealing with full decks, the decks are divided by halves. For example, let's go back to our single deck game. There are two half-decks in every full deck; that's easy to figure out.

We saw that approximately 2.5-3.0 cards are dealt to each participant in each round. Even if we lose track of how many cards have been dealt out, we can easily determine when the deck is halfway depleted by eyeballing the cards in the discard pile. More and more casinos, in single deck play, have the dealer place the discards already played to one side in an open plastic box.

Practice at home dealing out cards to yourself and a couple of imaginary other players as well as the dealer, and sweep up the discards after each round and place them to one side. With four participants, including the dealer, each round will use up approximately ten cards. With the burned card, that makes eleven cards. That's close enough to a 1/4 of a deck. Study how these cards look to the naked eye. To get a more exact look, purchase the same Bicycle cards the casinos use.

After a short while of dealing and observing, you'll easily know by the discard pile just when a half-deck has been depleted.

THE IMPORTANCE OF A TRUE COUNT

Why do we insist on a true, rather than a running count? Because it enables us to see more clearly the strength or weakness of the cards remaining. Here's an example.

Let's say we're counting cards, and playing with one other player against the dealer. At the end of the first round of play, the count (running count) is +2. This means that two more 10s are in the deck than 3s, 4s, 5s and 6s taken as a group. If eight cards were already dealt, it probably means that four small cards and two tens were played out.

Since the deck started with sixteen 10-value cards and sixteen small cards (3-4-5-6) there now remain fourteen 10s and twelve small cards. Even though the ratio is favorable, there are still plenty of small cards out.

But if thirty cards were dealt out, with the same resulting +2 running count, the deck will hold approximately ten 10s and eight small cards. It's a much better deck for the player now, with fewer small cards to worry about, and ten 10s still there.

The true count enables you to see more clearly the strength or weakness of the cards remaining.

To reflect this difference, if we divided the two half-decks (one full deck) after the first round of play into the +2 count, we'd come up with +1 true count. It's simply +2 divided by 2 = +1.

However, when we're down to a half deck, by dividing +2 by 1/2, we get a +4 figure. As the deck continues to be penetrated, assuming the running count remains the same at +2, the deck gets more and more favorable for us. Let's say there were only eight cards remaining. There now may be three 10s and only one 3 in the deck. Very strong!

Since we have only two half-decks to think about in a single deck, it becomes relatively easy to see the strength of the remaining cards, or, conversely, their weakness.

After the halfway mark has been reached, if you have a dealer who continues to penetrate the deck, that is, deal further into the deck, your plus count gets stronger and stronger, and you can reflect this strength in bigger and bigger bets. We'll show you how to do this without prompting casino heat.

For now, we're concentrating on single deck games. They're the easiest to play in terms of a count. The multiple deck games, which will require knowing that there are from four to twelve half-decks, are slightly more difficult, but can be mastered with just a bit of practice.

11

SINGLE DECK TRUE COUNT STRATEGY

INTRODUCTION

At the outset of play, we make a neutral bet. We suggest two units, or two chips. You may be comfortable in a $1 game at the beginning of your blackjack career, in which case you'll find a $1 minimum game and bet $2 as your first bet. As inflation rears its ugly head, you may find a single dollar table rare and far-between, but there are plenty of $2 minimum tables around. In which case, bet double $2, or $4 as your opening, neutral bet.

In a $5 game, your opening bet would be $10 ($5 x 2) and in a $25 game, it would be $50. If you can afford to play $100 stakes, your initial bet will be $200. It really doesn't matter what you bet, as long as you use our formula. Two units as the first, neutral bet.

If the deck becomes unfavorable, you reduce that bet to one unit. If the deck stays neutral, or even, the bet stays at two units.

We don't play hunches in 21; we play to win money, and we bet sanely. If the deck is unfavorable, the chances are that we're going to lose the next round of play, so we bet the minimum. There will be times that we'll get a blackjack out of the blue, but most of the time, we'll be a loser, and we want to lose only that minimum bet.

When the deck gets favorable, we increase our wager. Any favorability triggers this increase. The least favorable deck would be a +1 after the first round of play. Let's assume that we're playing with three other players (plus the dealer) and thus about 12.5 (let's call it 13) cards are dealt out in the first round of play.

The deck is +1. We know that theoretically one ace should be dealt for each 13 cards. That would be a neutral ratio. But two aces were dealt out. This is unfavorable. We take this into consideration and still make a neutral bet. The +1 has been balanced by the extra ace out of the deck.

Let's now assume that no aces were dealt on the first 13 cards and the deck is +1. We bet three units.

Here's a good method of increasing our bets. If the deck is +1 or +2 after the first round of play, with about 13 cards already played out, we increase out bet by one unit. If no aces have been dealt out yet, we bet four units.

If after half the deck has been dealt out, and the *true count* is +2 and the aces are neutral (two played out) we make a four unit wager. If we win this bet and the dealer continues to deal, and the deck is at least +2 with a true count, we increase our wager to six units to take full advantage of the situation.

STRATEGIC BET RAISING

Why this rule? If we lose our previous bet and then make a six unit wager, several things may happen. The dealer will probably shuffle up or bring attention to the wager so that a floorman will now get involved, for this kind of bet is made by only two types of players—card counters and *steamers*. By **steamers**, we mean a player who's been losing and goes wild, or as poker players say **on tilt**. He bets big to win back his previous losses with no regard to counts or favorabilities or anything else. He's out of control.

Since we're not steaming, a big bet now, after a loss, means we're counting cards. The average 21 player isn't a smart or skillful player. He cuts back after losses and increases bets after wins. You'll see this time and time at the table.

For example, you might see all four aces and a multitude of 10s out, for the players have hit blackjacks and 20s on the first round. The dealer is still dealing out cards, and while you've scaled your bet down to a minimum, here are others tripling their previous bets! Then moaning as they're dealt a 9-5 and the dealer shows a 2. Let's now summarize our method of betting:

SINGLE DECK: TRUE COUNT BETTING

SINGLE DECK: TRUE COUNT BETTING

Before the First Round of Play:
Neutral Bet of 2 units.

With 1/4 of Deck Depleted:
Count Neutral = 2 unit bet.
Count Negative = 1 unit bet.
Count +1 and aces neutral = 3 unit bet.
Count +1 and aces positive = 4 unit bet.
Count +2 and aces neutral = 4 unit bet.
Count +3 or more = 5 unit bet.

Half the Deck Depleted:
Count Negative = 1 unit bet.
Count +1 and aces unfavorable = 2 unit bet.
Count Neutral = 2 unit bet.
Count +2 and aces neutral = 4 unit bet
Count +3 or more and aces neutral = 6 unit bet

Further Penetration of Deck:
Count Negative = 1 unit bet.
Count Neutral and aces neutral = 2 unit bet.
Count Neutral and aces unfavorable = 1 unit bet
Count Neutral and aces favorable = 3 unit bet.
Count +1 and aces neutral = 4 unit bet
Count +1 and aces favorable = 5 unit bet
Count +2 or more, no regard to aces = 6 unit bet

If the previous hand won at 4 units, and the count is +2 or more, make a 6 unit bet.

ACES AND THE COUNT

It's possible to have a counting system where aces are included. If that were the case then all 10s and the aces would be -1, and the 2-3-4-5-6 would be +1. Although this is simpler, there are situations in single deck games where it is valuable to know the exact number of aces remaining in the deck, so we prefer the separate count of aces. Let me give you an actual situation that happened to me.

I was playing head-to-head against a dealer who dealt deeply into the deck, almost down to the last ten cards. The deck was slightly favorable, +1, but all four aces were still undealt, so I had a terrific situation with abut fourteen cards left to deal.

I put out a maximum bet of six units, and was dealt an 8-3. The dealer showed a 10. He peeked to see if he had an ace underneath, and amazingly, he didn't. I now had what is ordinarily an automatic double down of 11. But now there were only about ten cards left, and none of the four cards dealt to me or the dealer contained an ace. Which meant that of the ten cards remaining, four were aces. I had a 40% chance of getting an ace if I doubled down.

If I had a 10 to double down, that would be great, but an ace on an 11 would be brutal, almost a sure loser, and that meant a loss of 12 units instead of the six I had out.

I hesitated. As I did so, I turned my cards so the dealer could see my 8-3. Since many players who are unskilled don't like to double down an 11 against a dealer's 10, my hesitation conveyed this impression, not what I was really thinking, which was, *four aces in the deck; a double down is treacherous here*. I hit instead of doubling down and got an ace. Now I had a hard 12. I hit again, and got another ace! Hard 13. I hit again and got another ace! Hard 14.

"Where are these aces coming from?" I asked aloud. As if I didn't know. Now there were seven cards left in the deck. One of them was an ace. The deck was now still +1, since my 3 and the dealer's 10 balanced each other.

If it was +1 with seven cards left, I figured there were three 10s left and two small cards, and one neutral card, a 2, 7, 8 or 9.

Again I hesitated, and started thinking. I hadn't seen many 7s, only one actually. I had an 8-3 and been dealt three other 8s in the course of play. Maybe there were three 7s among the remaining neutral cards. Maybe. I hit and get a 6, the next-to-the last small card remaining in the deck. I had a 20. The dealer turned over his hole card. He had a 10 for 20. It was a hard push, but a push anyway.

My unit bets were $25 chips. Six of them amounted to $150. Doubling down would make the bet $300, and I'd have lost if I doubled down. If I had been counting the other way, with the 2 as a + card and the ace as a - card, the count would have been positive, I would have certainly doubled down.

That's why I like the ace as a special count. It still allows me to keep a solid count and know if there's a good chance of a blackjack, and at the same time it gives me that extra bit of information for just such a move as not doubling down on an 11.

SQUEEZING OUT FINAL B TION

We suggest sitting in either the **anchorman's** position at the table (the last seat) or the seat to the right of the anchorman (next to last seat). There is good reason for this. By sitting at the far end of the table, other players will have acted on their hands,

> Sitting at the far end of the table tells you something about the other players hands, and enables you to have a better fix on the actual count.

and the cards they receive or the way they play their hand will tell you something about their total values, and enable you to have a better fix on the actual count.

Here's an example: You're the third baseman (anchorman) and there are three other players in the game. The count is +1 and you've been dealt an 8-2. The dealer shows a 9 as his upcard. This is the second round of play, so about 13 cards have already been played out on the first round. A +1 means there is one more 10 remaining in the deck than the total of 3s, 4s, 5s and 6s.

You correctly have a three-unit bet out. You're ready to double down, which is correct play of a 10 against a 9. However, you have the weakest of the hard 10s, for the best 10 to hold would be a 5-5 or 6-4, all horrible cards you don't want to get on your hard 10 after doubling down. But that's a minor consideration. The deck is still +1, and you can still double down.

The first baseman turns over a blackjack. Now the count goes down to even, and the ace he turns over is the second dealt out, making the aces slightly weak. You want an ace if possible on your hard 10!

The second player hits and gets a 10, hits again, another 10, and turns over his cards. He has busted, originally holding Ace-2. So now the deck is suddenly -2, and three aces are out. The aces are negative now. The third player hits, gets a 10, hits again and turns over his bust hand of Ace-5-10-10. The deck is now -3 with no aces left. You're an underdog if you double down. You won't get an ace for a lock.

With a -3 deck, you're probably going to get a card from a 3-6 to give you a stiff weak total. If the dealer has an 8 or higher, he stands with his total and wins double your original bet. So here, the correct move is to merely hit the hand. You do so and get a 3 for a 13. You hit again and get a 5. The total you have is now 18, so you stand. The dealer turns over an 8 for a 17, and you win your original bet instead of losing double that bet.

COLLECTING INFORMATION

We'll show in the next section the deviations from Basic Strategy that occur because of the count. For purposes of this section, we show how important it is to get every bit of information you can before you make your move at the table.

So, when counting, pay attention to what is happening on the round you're about to make a decision on, such as splitting or doubling down, or even deciding whether to hit or stand.

For example, the following happened to me. The deck was +1, and I had a 3 unit bet out. I was dealt a 9-6 for a hard 15. The dealer showed a 10. I got ready to hit the hand, but two players were to act in front of me. One hit and got a 3, hit again and got a 4, hit again and got a 6! Now he counted up his cards and shoved his hole cards under his chips. He could only have an 8 total in his hole cards at best, and possibly a 5-3 or 6-2. Even if I credited him with the 6-2, the deck had now gone from +1 to +5.

The next player hit, got a 6 and shoved his cards under his chips. He probably had a hard 12 or better to stand, and so the deck increased conservatively to +6. Five cards that could help me were now on the table. If I hit the 15 I was a goner. So I stood.

The dealer, miracle of miracles, turned over a 2 as his hole card, for a 10-2, hit and got a 10, and busted. I won by a hair.

Of course, not all my blackjack plays turned out this well, but I was able to take advantage of information to make an intelligent decision. If I make the right decision and lose, well, that's the game. But If I make a wrong decision and lose because of it, then I feel stupid. I don't want to feel stupid, and neither do you. Squeeze out everything you can before making your decision. In the long run, good fortune follows good play.

SINGLE DECK: ALTERING PLAY ACCORDING TO THE COUNT

When we refer to a count, it is a **true count**. In single-deck games, where there are only two half-decks, it's easy to eyeball the discards or to use our formula of 2.5 cards per participant per round. Round it off to 3 cards per participant if 2.5 throws you off.

As the deck gets penetrated, the changed plays become stronger. Here are changes to keep in mind.

Most of the original moves recommended by Basic Strategy affecting these hands are moves that give the player just a small, minimal advantage over the casino. Therefore, changes in the count, either + or -, cause alterations in strategy.

SINGLE DECK:
PLUS COUNT ALTERATION CHART

A. If the true count is +1 or more:

Hitting vs Standing
- Don't hit a hard 12 against a dealer's 2 or 3
- Don't hit a hard 16 against a dealer's 10

Insurance
- If at least one-quarter of the deck is played out, and the dealer shows an ace, take insurance.

Doubling down
- Double down a soft 18 against a dealer's 2*
- Double down a soft 19 against a dealer's 5*

* Both of these are expert plays that may draw casino heat. This factor must be taken into consideration.

SINGLE DECK:
MINUS COUNT ALTERATION CHART

B. If the true count is -1 or more:

Hitting vs. Standing
- Hit a hard 12 against a dealer's 4.
- Hit a hard 13 against a dealer's 2 or 3.
- Hit a soft 18 against a dealer's ace.
- Never double down on Ace-2.

Doubling Down
- Double down on Ace-3 only against the 6.
- Double down on Ace-4 and Ace-5 only against the dealer's 5-6.
- Double down on Ace-6 and Ace-7 only against the dealer's 4-5-6.
- Never double down on Ace-8.
- Never double down on hard 8.
- Double down on hard 9 only against the dealer's 5 and 6.
- Double down on hard 10 against the dealer's 2-8.
- Double down on hard 11 against the dealer's 2-9.

Splitting Pairs
- Split 2s only when the dealer has 4-7.
- Split 3s only when the dealer has 5-7.
- Split 6s only when the dealer has 5-6.
- Do not split 9s against a dealer's 3.

As we can readily see, the changes made with - hands considerably overwhelm those made with + hands. Study them carefully and play out hands till you have them pat.

Basically, what is happening is this—with a minus deck the chances of getting small cards are greater and therefore will hurt a number of our double down and splitting situations. It's common sense, and by understanding this instead of blindly memorizing the changes, you'll have a better idea of why you're making these altered moves and will be able, in actual casino situations, to develop a sixth sense.

We showed you in a previous example how four aces in a penetrated deck forced us to alter our strategy and not double down a hard 11 against a dealer's 10. This is unusual, but knowing the situation, I took advantage of it.

THE FANTASY CASINO

Here's another interesting situation. Suppose you're playing head-to-head against the dealer, and there are only six cards left in the deck. On this day your mind is clear and you're very sharp. You're keeping track of all cards, and realize the six cards remaining consist of four 8s and two 7s. In this fantasy situation, you're at a casino where you can bet anything you want anytime. What do you bet on the next hand?

The answer is—everything you own in the world. You can't lose. No matter what you're dealt, you stand. The dealer must bust if he hits his hand. It's a sure thing.

You'll either get a 14, 15 or 16. The dealer will get the same kind of hand, but since there's no card smaller than a 7 to draw to if he has a 15 or 16, he must bust. If he has a 14, only 8s remain in the deck and he must bust.

Once you play single-deck blackjack and master our simple but effective count, you can then keep track of other cards, eyeball them if you will. The 7s, 8s and 9s can be seen as cards that are in the deck or played out. If these cards are in the deck, then your hitting of a 12 can be more aggressive. It's a good hit against the dealer's 4, if you have a big chance of getting a 7, 8 or 9.

If the aces are in the deck, your hard total of 10 becomes stronger as a doubling down card. Give yourself leeway when playing single-deck for those moments when you can keep track of a lot of cards. Don't play hunches, of course, and don't go against Basic Strategy unless you know the situation is ripe for it.

If you want to stick to Basic Strategy alone, and count cards, then just follow our rules and deviations according to the count. You'll win without taxing your mind.

12

MULTIPLE DECK
TRUE COUNT STRATEGY

INTRODUCTION

Once we go beyond a single deck, it is greatly to our advantage to know the true count. To get the true count, we use the half-deck principle, there being two half-decks per single deck. Thus, in a two deck game, there are four half-decks; in a four deck game, eight half-decks, and with a six deck game, 12 half-decks.

Whatever our count during the first round of play in a multiple deck game, that is, our running count, is divided by the half-decks remaining. For example, let's say you're at a four deck game with one other player.

On the first round of play, you are dealt a 10-6, hit and get a 7. The other player hits a 4-2, gets a 6, hits again, gets a 5 and stands with a hard 17. The dealer's upcard was a 9. He has a 5 in the hole and hits and gets a 4.

The running count is +5. Ten cards have been played out, (a little more than our theoretical 2.5 cards per player per round). We haven't even gotten through half a deck. Since there are 8 half-decks in our four-deck game, we divide +5 by 7. We come up with a total of less than +1. Of course, we won't have a calculator at the table, but we know instinctively that any number divided by a larger number gives us a result less than 1.

We keep playing as if the deck were neutral, since the true count is less than +1, even though the running count is positive. As the game goes on, after eight rounds of play, three half-decks have been depleted. Our running count is +7. Since only five half-decks remain, we can see that the true count is hovering around +1.5. That's easy to calculate.

After eight more rounds of play, we find that only two half-decks remain. If our running count is now +10, we divide that by 2 (our remaining half-decks) and come up with a +5 true count, a very powerful total for us.

PRACTICE ESTIMATING HALF DECKS

Practice this kind of counting by dealing out cards to yourself. Do it slowly till you familiarize yourself with the remaining half-decks in the game. Put varying amount of decks to one side, one set on top of the other, so that by eyeballing the discards you can tell approximately how many half decks have been used up. Count the discards to verify your count.

After a little practice you should be able to tell just how many half-decks remain.

THE CHIP TECHNIQUE

To aid you further, assume for simplicity's sake that each participant in the game gets 3 cards per round of play. That's not exact, but close enough for your calculations in a multiple deck game. If there are four participants, then 12 cards are going out each round, almost a half-deck each two rounds. That's easy to figure. You can keep some chips put aside to keep track of the rounds played.

For example, you keep placing one chip on another, separate from your piles of chips, just to know how many rounds have been played out. If you have ten chips, that's five half-decks depleted. That would leave three half-decks in a four-deck game. So, whatever your running count, you divide by 3 to get your true count.

If you can do it without chips, fine. But make sure you know the true count in a multiple deck game. That's your key to correct betting and correct play.

MULTIPLE DECK RUNNING COUNT

As you can readily see, in any multiple deck game, whether it be four or six decks, the true count starts well below +1, even if there's a + running count, unless that running count begins at an extremely large level.

For example, if you're playing six deck blackjack, and the running count goes to +4 right away with 11 half-decks remaining, you've gotten a very slight favorable situation, not enough to alter your bet or your play.

With this in mind, let's see how we alter our wagers according to a true count.

> *Make sure you know the true count in a multiple deck game. That's your key to correct betting and correct play.*

MULTIPLE DECK: ALTERING BETS ACCORDING TO TRUE COUNT

Unlike single deck games, where we recommend a neutral bet of two units, which will usually be double the minimum bet allowed at a table, in a multiple deck game we start with just a one-unit wager until the true count gets to at least +1.

Whenever the decks are negative, neutral or less than +1, our only bet is that one-unit. You'll have to be patient in multiple deck games. Sometimes all six decks will be depleted without you increasing your wager. But your patience will pay off in the end.

At some point, the decks will get favorable, and stay favorable, round after round. That's when you have to sock it in, and take advantage of their favorability. Our watchword, then, in multiple deck games—*patience*.

INCREASING THE BET

When the decks finally reach +1 as a true count, we increase our betting to two units. Then we keep going higher and higher, and can reach ten or twelve units at times. In single-deck games, it's difficult to go from a neutral bet of two units to eight units without drawing heat, but in multiple deck games we can slide way up on the scale.

The increase is gradual, and the decks take a long time to be played out. There's no red flag even if you finally get up to ten or even 12 units. That's how most tourists play multiple deck games. When the going is good, they press their bets, whatever the count.

You can be most aggressive after winning a previous hand. Losing the hand shouldn't prevent you from making a bigger bet, but not as big as you would have made if you won the last hand.

You want to blend in with the other players, who generally raise bets after winning and lower or keep the same bet after a loss.

Let's say the deck is still favorable and you bet six units and won. You can easily drag two chips and make a ten unit bet, or even double your wager to 12 units. But if you lost the hand, and there's any danger of casino heat or a floorman is lingering nearly, then increase it to just eight units.

You want to blend in with the other players, who generally raise bets after winning and lower or keep the same bet after a loss. They don't care about the count. They play the **rush**, a lucky streak.

MULTIPLE DECK: TRUE COUNT BETTING

One caveat before going on. In double deck games, bet less aggressively than in the multiple deck four and six deck games because, like the single deck games, too wide a spread between a minimum and maximum bet may draw casino heat.

We'll show this in the tables.

MULTIPLE DECK:
TRUE COUNT BETTING CHARTS

Two Deck True Count Betting:

Deck (True Count)	Bet
Minus	1 Unit
+ (less than +1)	1 Unit
+1	2 Units
+2 to +3	3 Units
+4	4 Units
+5 or more	6 Units -Upper limit

Four - Six Deck True Count Betting:

Deck (True Count)	Bet
Minus	1 Unit
+ (less than +1)	1 Unit
+1	2 Units
+2 to +3	3 Units
+4	4 Units
+5	6 Units
+6	6 Units
+7	8 Units
+8	10 Units
+9 and above	12 Units-Upper limit

Note that we play a 1-6 unit game with double decks and a 1-12 unit game with 4-6 decks. If there's no heat, and a co-operative casino or dealer, then you can increase the double-deck units to 8, and the 4-6 decks units to 15.

MULTIPLE DECK: ALTERING PLAY ACCORDING TO THE COUNT

Multiple Deck Plus Count Alteration Chart

If the True Count is +1 or More

Hitting vs. Standing

- Stand with hard 12 vs. 2 or 3.
- Stand with hard 16 vs. a 10.
- Stand with 7-7 vs. a 10.
- Stand with Ace-7 vs. a 10.

Splitting Pairs With a +1 Count

- Split 2s vs. a 3.
- Split 6s vs. a 2.

Insurance

- Take insurance with a + 2 count.

MULTIPLE DECK:
MINUS COUNT ALTERATION CHART

If the True Count is -1 or More

Hitting vs. Standing
- Hit hard 13 vs. a 3.
- Hit 7-7 vs. a 10.

Doubling Down With a + Count
- Double down a 8 vs. 5-6
- Double down a 9 vs. 2-3.
- Double down an 11 vs. an Ace.
- Double down Ace-2 vs. 4.
- Double down Ace-3 vs. 4.
- Double down Ace-6 vs. 2.
- Double down Ace-7 vs. 2.
- Double down Ace-8 vs. 5-6.

Don't Double With a - Count
- Don't double down 9 vs. 4.
- Don't double down 10 vs. 9.
- Don't double down Ace-2 vs. 5-6.
- Don't double down Ace-3 vs. 5.
- Don't double down Ace-4 vs. 4.
- Don't double down Ace-5 vs. 4.
- Don't double down Ace-6 vs. 3.
- Don't double down Ace-7 vs. 3.

Splitting Pairs
- Don't Split 3s vs. 4-5.
- Don't Split 6s vs. 3-4.
- Don't Split 9s vs. 2-3.

KEEPING TRACK OF ACES

Just as with single deck play, aces play an important role in multiple deck card counting. Since there are four aces per deck, the normal distribution of aces should be two per half-deck. When less than two aces are dealt out per half-deck, the decks remaining are **ace-rich**; conversely, if more than two aces go out per half-deck, the decks are **ace-poor**.

When the decks are ace-rich and the true count is +1, then you can bet a bit more aggressively. When the decks are ace-rich but minus, there is no change. However, should there be a slight plus value, such as +1 or less than +1, bet more aggressively. With an ace-rich decks situation and the decks +1 or more, you can add an extra unit to your bet.

For example, if the decks are +1 with a true count, and after four half-decks only six, instead of 8 aces have been dealt, we recommend 3 units be bet instead of two. An easy way to work this is as follows:

> • If the deck is + but less than +1 and ace-rich, bet two units.
>
> • Anytime the decks are +2 or more and ace-rich, add one additional unit to your normal bet for that situation.

On the other hand, if the decks are ace-poor, then you bet more cautiously. If the decks are extremely ace-poor, that is, running two aces under normal distribution, such as only eight aces in five half-decks instead of the normal 10, then subtract one unit from your correct bet according to the true count.

This method requires a side-count of aces, but that can be done with chips or with your feet or fingers. Position chips, for example, so that it shows how many aces have been dealt out. Or use whatever method you find easiest to keep a side-count of the aces. This count will pay off for you, especially in blackjacks in ace-rich situations with big bets out there.

A SIMPLIFIED COUNT FOR MULTIPLE DECK GAMES

For those of you who desire to play a more leisurely game; whose main interest is to have fun while playing blackjack, we have come up with a simplified count. With this count, you don't have to keep track of aces as a separate entity. Here's how it works.

We give a value of +1 to the following cards: 2-3-4-5-6. We give a -1 value to the next set of cards: 10-value cards and aces. The following cards are neutral: 7-8-9

A side count of aces will pay off for you, especially in blackjacks in ace-rich situations with big bets out there

With this count we don't use a separate count of aces. We eliminate that aspect of the count, since aces are already built into the count. You still use the running count and divide it by half-decks to get the true count.

You increase your bets as with the regular true count, and you alter your basic strategy in the same manner, according to the true count.

USING THE RUNNING COUNT ALONE

If you find that keeping track of both running count and a true count involving half-decks interferes with your enjoyment of the game, but you still want to know if the decks are favorable or unfavorable, we've worked out this more simplified method of counting. Now we go strictly by a *running count*.

Here's what you must do. At the outset of play, start with a negative count.

Using Only the Running Count

• A two-deck game starts with -2.
• A four-deck game starts with -4.
• A six-deck game starts with -6.

Keep making a minimum bet as long as the decks are negative or neutral. Use a running count, either the original count balancing 3-6s against 10s with a side count of aces, or if you want it more simplified, don't take a side count of aces and simply count 2-6 against the 10s and aces.

This way you can relax more while playing multiple deck blackjack and still have a good idea of how the decks stand, whether positive or negative.

Although this method isn't as accurate as our other methods of counting, it will give you a solid plan for raising or lowering your bets according to a count and allow you to alter your basic strategy.

13

MANAGING THE DEALER

INTRODUCTION

Theoretically, the dealer is just a tool of the casino, a sort of robot who does the duties he or she is paid to do. The dealer takes cash and gives out casino chips in return. The dealer shuffles the cards and deals them out, pays off winning bets and collects losing bets.

But the dealer's role is broader than that. If no tipping were allowed and if a robot was dealing , then the player wouldn't have to pay attention to the dealer. But the dealer can interpose himself or herself in a way that is either helpful or harmful to the player. So the player must be prepared to cope with the dealer's actions.

We're going to thoroughly cover the relationship of the dealer to the player. We're going to show you which dealers to play against and which to avoid. We're going to show you how to take advantage of a dealer *legally*. In this section we'll show you the warning signs of a harmful dealer, and the signs that point to a good dealer. You'll find out how to handle the dealer, how to establish a relationship that will be beneficial to you, the player.

HOW TO JUDGE A DEALER

What you basically want is a friendly dealer. An unfriendly, cold automaton who barely acknowledges your presence at the table when you sit down is going to cause you potential trouble. If you're about to sit down at a table against a dealer, and get bad vibes, it's no crime to get right up again. You don't have to give any excuses—you don't have to lie about your reason for leaving the table. Just leave.

What I've noticed in casinos is that even if the place is crowded, there'll be one or two tables that are completely empty. The dealer will be standing there, grimfaced, his or her arms folded across the chest. What you can be sure of is that the players who had been at that empty table were destroyed, and fled like rats from a sinking ship.

There have been times when my thought processes went like this—"ok, players have been killed at this table, but maybe the cards will turn. So, now, after the bad cards are out, I'm coming in fresh to a new deal of good cards." Everytime I thought this way and acted on that thought, I found my bankroll dislodged in a short period of time. It's happened so many times that I can become paranoid and think that the cards are stacked so that I just can't win.

I might start playing one hand—then switch to two hands to break up the terrible rhythm of the cards. Nothing helps.

Usually the dealer, still grimfaced, just keeps taking away my chips without a gesture to

You want a friendly dealer, not an unfriendly, cold automaton who barely acknowledges your presence.

157

indicate *bad luck; that's the fourth time your 20 lost to my 21, and I can also think of the 2s and 3s I deal to all your hard double-downs*.

PLAYING EMPTY TABLES

So, the first rule is—avoid an empty table in an otherwise crowded casino if the dealer has a grim look and has his arms crossed across his chest. That kind of body language is going to be poor comfort for your bankroll. Sometimes, since I'm anxious to play head-to-head, rather than at a crowded table, I'll be patient. When the dealer goes "on break," I sit down to a fresh face.

This doesn't mean that I always avoid empty tables. If the dealer isn't angry looking I might sit down. Perhaps my feeling about empty tables and grim dealers is irrational, but I've been burned so many times, it's a rule of thumb with me to avoid that combination.

Some dealers prefer not to show emotion. That's ok. I figure they've been dealing to losers all day or night, and are constantly getting blamed for the cards they deal out by these angry players so many try to have a neutral demeanor.

The first thing I do when sitting down and getting ready to play is to note the name of the dealer, and in some casinos where the information is given on a nametag, the place the dealer comes from originally.

So, I sit down and say "Ron, how's the table been?"

I've spoken and I expect a verbal answer. Any answer is all right. "

Not bad." Or "so-so."

Or "I seem to be real lucky." But what I don't like is

a shrug of the shoulders as if my presence isn't worth a reply. That to me is an angry overture.

THE ROLE OF THE DEALER

Before going any further, we should examine the role of the dealer in a casino. In many instances, he's paid to do a job competently. Fine. In others, he's there to make sure no one wins, and if he suspects a card counter or skillful player, he signals a floorman. Even if a player is not skilled but winning, he signals a floorman.

Sometimes this attitude reflects the whole casino. Sometimes it reflects the shift the dealer is working on, run by a shift boss or pit boss. And sometimes, it's just the attitude of a dealer who's angry with the world.

I want a smiling friendly dealer, someone whom I can talk to while playing. Someone who responds. If I don't get this, then I will leave the table unless I'm winning steadily. Anything else and I'm gone and gone fast.

GETTING INFORMATION FROM THE DEALER

A dealer, particularly at a casino where he or she must examine the hole card if the upcard is a 10 or ace, can give away a lot of information to the player by the way he or she peeks. Some give away nothing. I was once at a downtown casino playing head-to-head with a dealer who was at least six foot four. Standing erect, he could pick up the corner of his hole card and somehow know its value in an instant. He was impossible to read.

Other dealers have **tells**, that is, giveaways of the value of the cards they're peeking at. If a dealer sees a 10 or **paint** (jack, queen or king) the moment the card in the hole is turned slightly, it's apparent what value that card is. If the card is a small card, most particularly the 4, the hole card must be lifted more to see its value. Sometimes the 4, which most resembles the ace, causes the dealer to turn up the card a couple of times, to verify whether or not he has a blackjack when his upcard is a 10.

So that is something to observe. Most of the time you play you'll get no information from an experienced dealer. Sometimes you'll get a lot. A dealer may be experienced, but since you've treated him like a human being, he's trying to be helpful to you. After all, the major income of a dealer is from **tokes** or **tips**. If you're winning, you will usually tip more. If the dealer is helpful, you will tip more.

What I really mean is—if the dealer is friendly and helpful, tip the dealer. Put him on your side all the way. On the other side of the coin, there are dealers who go out of their way to be unfriendly and unhelpful. Here's an example.

I was playing with one other player at a $25 table. I was doing well, and the dealer was getting more and more annoyed. Maybe he had a losing table all of his shift and was worried about heat from his bosses. Whatever his reasons, he was there to harass and annoy me, since I was really winning.

After several rounds of play, he dealt me a 10-6 and showed a 10 as his upcard. I waited for him to peek before making a decision. The deck was neutral and I had a neutral bet out, so I was prepared to hit the 16. He peeked at his hole card, repeeked again, holding the card up by the corner for an unnaturally long time. I thought—he's telling me something. Maybe his demeanor is just to impress his bosses.

So I stood. The dealer smirked and turned over a king of spades, perhaps the most blatant of the 10-value cards to see by all its paint. I didn't say anything. I looked at the dealer, and he stared into my eyes, a nasty stare. I sat there not making a bet, then once more stared at him, this time giving him my famous million yard stare, got up, and gathered up my chips.

"Want to change color?" he said, indicating my stacks of $25 chips which he wanted to change to $100 chips.

"You must be kidding," I said, and walked away, still boiling. I cashed in and left the casino. I don't play when I'm angry. A few days later I played in the same casino against a friendly dealer. So I guessed it was just that dealer who had a bug up his ass.

14

ADVANCED DEALER TIPS

Dealers, like all human beings, make mistakes. Since you're in a game where your money is at stake, you should take advantage of the mistakes. Casinos take advantage of players all the time; they ply them with liquor and will deal to a dead-drunk who doesn't know what he's doing. Or to a helpless novice who doesn't have the slightest idea of what blackjack is all about. So don't feel guilty about reversing the tables.

FIRST TIP: DEALER GIVES AWAY THE VALUE OF HIS HOLE CARD

A dealer can do this in several ways. In casinos where the dealer must look at his hole card when holding a 10 or ace as his upcard, to determine whether or not he has a blackjack, the player can gleam a great deal of information by watching how he peeks at the hole card.

a. Dealer Has a Stiff Card

When a dealer has a small stiff card, such as a 2, 3, 4, 5 or 6 in the hole, he may have to lift the card more than usual to ascertain that it isn't an ace. The most difficult card for him is a 4. Even experienced dealers lift the card one or twice when it's a 4.

Strategy: If the count is +, and you have a stiff total of 12-16, you'll stand and let the dealer go first, hoping he busts.

b. Dealer Has Paint

Conversely, this same kind of dealer quickly glances at his hole card when it is paint (jack, queen or king) or if it's a 7-8-9 or 10.

Strategy: If you have a stiff hard total, from 12 to 16, you must hit. If you're in a casino which permits surrender, surrender your hand from 12-16. If the deck or decks are negative, keep hitting even if you have a four card hard total.

c. First Basing

The dealer permits you to **first base**. **First basing** is named after the player in the first seat who sits at a hard angle to the dealer, and can see the dealer's hole card if the dealer is sloppy and lifts it incorrectly without protecting its value.

First basing is a tricky concept. If you happen to be in the first baseman's seat, and you see the dealer's hole card, then that's to your advantage. If you hire or station someone to sit or stand either in the seat or behind it to first base, the casino will consider this cheating and may take measures including detaining or arresting you.

Strategy: So, if you're first basing, be careful, even if you're doing it legitimately as a result of the dealer's ignorance. Knowing the dealer's actual upcard gives you a big advantage over the house. Again, if the dealer holds a high stiff such as a 4-5-6, you'll stand with all stiff totals no matter what the count. If the deck is +, you'll stand with all your stiff hands of hard 12-16.

Holding soft hands, you won't allow yourself to bust. You'll hit all soft 18s, since you can only improve the hand and not bust at best, and at worst, you'll end up with a weaker hard total which shouldn't bother you. You figure the dealer has a good chance of busting. For example, if you know by first basing or by the dealer's peek that he has a stiff card in the hole, with a 10 as his upcard, and you hold an Ace-7, the correct Basic Strategy is to hit. So you hit.

However, if you're first basing and know the dealer holds a 7 in the hole for a hard 17, you stand on your soft 18. That makes sense. Your 18 is a winner. Why tamper with it?

If the deck is -2 or more and the dealer holds a 2 or 3, you'll hit your hard 12, 13 and 14, but not the 15 or 16. If the deck was neutral or positive, then you'll stand with any stiff total.

SECOND TIP:
DEALER MAKES INCORRECT PAYOUT

Dealers make mistakes. We know that. Don't always take the dealer's payout for granted. He or she may have been working a long shift and now is at the end of it. You've had a $75 bet out and gotten a blackjack, and now are paid off. It's a tricky payout at 3-2, amounting to $112.50. Make sure you get the full amount. You'll usually be paid off with four $25 chips, two $5 chips, two $1 chips and 50¢. Get everything.

If the dealer pays you too much, the decision is yours as to whether you'll call attention to the incorrect payout. The only one that loses is the house, not the dealer personally. It's not like being in a small store where the cashier gives you change for $20 when you gave her a $10 bill. At the end of the day, the poor woman may have to make up the difference out of her own pocket. Here, the game goes on.

THIRD TIP: DEALER IS IN COLLUSION WITH ANOTHER PLAYER AT THE TABLE

I've seen this a few times. I was once at a downtown casino in the early morning hours and playing at a double deck game. The reason the game interested me in the first place was that the sole occupant of the table had a huge pile of chips in front of him, sloppily placed as if he had a pyramid in front of him. This was very unusual, and should have been a red flag to the dealer or floorman. I sat down in the seat next to third base.

The player was two seats away. I cashed in a couple of hundred dollars (it was a $5 table) and made a bet of $5 without knowing the count. The decks were almost depleted. I won the first hand as did the player.

The cards were reshuffled. They were given to the player to cut. There was a glance I caught between them; as though I had interrupted something. It's the same look you see when you stumble upon a friend talking to a woman he has something with. You're in the way; you see how they look at each other, so you pack up and go. But I wanted to see what this was all about.

It was about 3:30 A.M. and I had nothing better to do. I was living in Vegas and used the 24-hour town as my oyster. I was up and about at all hours. Nothing happened for the first three rounds of play. The player stood when the dealer showed a 10. I hit my hard 14 and busted. The dealer turned over a stiff hole card and busted, then turned over the player's two cards. The player had stood on a hard 12!

And this player, a young guy with a hard look about him, was betting big. He shoveled the last chips he received on his pyramid. Then he was dealt a blackjack, and pushed his cards across his chips, when turning over the cards. A player can't go near his chips once a hand is dealt. What he had done was **past post**, that is, by keeping some chips in the palm of his hand, he pushed his palm open and dropped the chips onto the stack of chips he had just bet, increasing their value after the fact.

Strategy: This was really something. The dealer would have to be blind not to see that one. Now, I started making bigger bets. What I would do, I decided, was mimic the player.

I couldn't quite see his cards, but I noticed that there was eye contact between him and the dealer on some hands, and none on others. The eye contact came only at certain times when the dealer showed a 10 or ace as his upcard. Thus it came after he peeked. He was giving the player a signal, which I picked up after another ten minutes. And I could see the player was also keeping the count, and really making big bets when it was plus. He seemed to have a no lose situation.

I looked around. The floorman, a florid character in a

wild checkered jacket and wilder shirt, was chatting up a bored cocktail waitress at the end of the pit. No heat here at this hour. Now that I caught the signal, I started making the same offbeat plays, hitting and standing seemingly at random, doubling down with crazy soft totals, and winning.

Without ever saying a word to the dealer or other player, I played for almost an hour at the table and won $700, then left, leaving them doing their same waltz.

LAST TIP: THE DEALER THINKS HE CAN SPOT A COUNTER AND DECIDES ON HIS OWN TO TAKE COUNTERMEASURES.

Usually, when I'm at a table where the dealer shuffles up every time I make a bigger bet, I say nothing and simply walk away. Why bother with these bastards? But sometimes I decide to have a bit of fun, and try to outsmart the ignoramus who really doesn't know what the count is, but is going simply by the player's bet.

Strategy: What I do is this—whenever the deck is neutral or positive, I have a neutral big bet out. When the deck gets negative, I increase the bet. I've seen counters fighting the dealer by raising the bet with the count and having the dealer shuffle up while they sat there and cursed. The hell with cursing.

At a Strip casino single-deck game, I did this act against not only a dealer but a floorman, both watching my action. It was a $25 table with good rules, standing on all 17s, doubling down after pair splitting, etc. I started with a $100 bet and kept that bet when the deck was neutral or favorable. Unfavorable—I raised it to $200 and got the cards shuffled up. Sometimes I got stuck, for the dealer wouldn't shuffle up after but one round. It took two rounds. For the most part, however, I killed the game.

The two jerks couldn't figure out what was happening. They didn't know how to count—they just blindly went along with my scam. That night I really won big. A real pleasure.

TIPPING THE DEALER

Tipping or **toking**, as the casino pros call it, is a fairly standard practice in American casinos. Dealers probably make at least 3/4 of their income from tokes. The casinos pay them little and they're always looking for the big tipper, whom they call a *George*. A lousy tipper is designated as a *Tom*, as in Tom Turkey. Of course, those terms aren't standard around the country, but be aware that the dealer wants tips.

Some card counters never tip a dealer. They're really hard-bitten cheapskates at heart, and each toke they give away is another chip they can't pocket. These are the kinds of players who get barred and who are always whining and complaining about casino heat. But they bring it upon themselves. They're so cold and impersonal that to them, the dealer is a robot without feelings, there to deal and pay off their winnings. Then, after five minutes of play, these characters feel the warm hand of a security guard on their shoulders and are told to move along.

I believe in tipping the dealer. I don't tip elaborately but at crucial moments. I tip more when a dealer is helpful and I'm winning, than when he's helpful and I'm losing. That's natural and the dealer understands this. But if the dealer is cooperating with me, and I'm getting good cards, he's going to be steadily tipped.

HOSTILE DEALERS

If a dealer is hostile, don't tip him. If a dealer goes out of his way to throw you off, don't tip him. If a dealer rushes the game or slows the game (either one) so that you're uncomfortable, don't put out a toke. In fact, just leave the table unless you're on a rush—winning everything in sight.

I had this situation against a really hostile woman, all aglitter with gold rings and gold necklaces and a gold and diamond Rolex. To her, I was just some lowlife sitting at her table. She was bored to death, never responded to anything pleasant I said to her except with a sneer and frown.

> *I believe in tipping the dealer. I don't tip excessively but at crucial moments.*

I hated her. And she dealt the cards with speed and thrust, so they were always hitting my knuckles. Once they went past me off the table. But there we were, head-to-head, and I couldn't lose. If she had an ace as her upcard and I had a hard 16, I hit a 5 and she lost. Every double down was a winner. I had started as a $50 player and now, after a half-hour, my neutral bet was $125, then $150, then $200. And still the cards came. Finally, she was relieved.

A new dealer came on, a guy who stared at my stack of chips with a look that said, "okay, yo-yo, wait till you see what I do to you."

Where did they get these dealers? He dealt himself a

blackjack and took away my first bet, which I had reduced to $50. Then I doubled down on an 11 and got a 2, while he converted a hard 16 into a winner. That was it. I let him change color, and he kept waiting for me to toke him, but no way.

> *The best dealers are those who co-operate, and you can make them co-operate by generous and correct toking.*

AVERAGE DEALERS

On the other hand, I've encountered dealers who, though they didn't give an inch as far as rules went, were human beings. We could talk and pass the time. Everything wasn't involved with an effort to have me lose. I'd tip these dealers with average tokes.

THE BEST DEALERS

The best dealers are those who co-operate, and you can make them co-operate by generous and correct toking. Here's an example.

I was playing a single-deck game against a woman dealer who was telling me about her two kids. She had been divorced in the East, and come out to Vegas to visit a woman friend, and decided to become a dealer and start a new life. In Philadelphia, she told me, at best she'd have become a secretary at one-third the money she was making now.

A common story in Vegas. People looking for a fresh start, a new career, better weather, better schools. She asked if I was a local—I told her I had been living in Vegas for six months, that I was writing a book. Did I write novels? I told her I did, and wrote down my name on a piece of paper with a list of my books. And we continued playing.

It was a single deck game. She dealt down about two-thirds, which was good. This is called **penetration**. A friend of mine suggested that gambling was much like life, the deeper the penetration, the better the situation. Well, take it any way you will. I didn't tell the dealer this, of course.

As the deck moved along the one round, it got more and more favorable. The count was something like +7 and three aces were left. A juicy situation. I wanted the dealer to penetrate more deeply than she had been doing. So I made a big bet and a big tip, putting the tip right in the betting box where I could leave it for still another round. "Let's win this together , " I said to her. "I have a feeling about the next hand."

She hesitated. She would normally shuffle up here, but taking my suggestion, dealt me another hand, a blackjack. Beautiful. Her $10 tip became $25.

"One more time," I said. Again she hesitated, but in the end, dealt me another hand. I had two 10s. She showed a 7 as her upcard and stood on hard 17. Now there was $50 in tokes for her. All from the original $10 toke.

"Thanks," I said. "Here you are." I pushed the toke towards her. She smiled and thanked me, and was relieved about fifteen minutes later. But from that moment till she left the table, she shuffled up if I didn't put down a toke, and kept dealing if the toke was in the box. I didn't have to say anything—she knew what was going on.

ADVANCED TOKING – FIVE CONCEPTS

1 • If you're in a game where the dealer has discretion over his or her penetration of the deck, try to tip the dealer when you want her to continue to deal into a favorable deck.

To do this most effectively, place a bet in the betting box, where you control the bet. If you place the toke outside the box, if the bet is won, the dealer must remove the toke. If it's lost, it's lost along with your bet. But keeping it in the betting box allows you to control it. You can either hand it to the dealer or let it ride if the bet is won, and the dealer can't touch it.

If you've make a toke bet in the betting box and the dealer continues to deal, but the deck get unfavorable, than hand the tip to the dealer as a signal that she can now shuffle up.

If the deck remains favorable, keep the toke bet going. A good thing to say is "let's win this together," or words to that effect.

Even though dealers share tips, with the whole shift usually participating, they want those tokes, because the more each dealer gets, the more there is for everybody.

Dealers share tokes because sharing is more equitable. The dealers in the bigger games usually make the most in tokes; whereas the smaller games yield the least. This way, no matter what game the dealer deals, he or she knows the share will be equal at the end of the shift.

If you make a toke bet in the box and the dealer doesn't keep dealing, then remove the toke bet and just keep your own bet. Then try it again. If it still doesn't have the desired effect either you have an uncooperative dealer, or the dealer is afraid to bend the rules. If you are hurt by this, leave the table.

2 • A small toke is always welcome after you've been dealt a blackjack. It doesn't have to be much. I've found that a $1 or $2 bet out there for the dealer is okay. I never give a bet directly to the dealer; I always put it in the betting box. There may be exceptions, however. Sometimes, if I'm real friendly with the dealer, I'll ask if she wants the toke directly or

> *I never give a bet directly to the dealer; I always put it in the betting box.*

wants me to bet it for her. Usually, they want it bet, but sometimes a dealer will want it directly. So I give it to her. Why go against her feelings?

3 • If the dealer is being helpful even though I'm not getting great cards, I never complain to the dealer or blame her. And I still tip, especially if the deck is favorable, and I have a big bet out. In fact, anytime I have a big bet out at a juncture where the cards may or may not be reshuffled, I put a toke bet out. I want another round of cards dealt.

4 • Even when dealers can't control the shuffle point, such as multiple deck games dealt from a shoe, where the shuffle card comes up arbitrarily, I toke the dealers to keep them friendly. If I'm a card counter and playing skillfully, I don't want an expert move, such as a double down of a soft 19 against the dealer's 6, brought to the attention of the floorman. I don't want any attention, period.

If a dealer signals a floorman to come over and watch my play, then I will not toke the dealer, nor leave the table immediately. If the deck is unfavorable at this point, I will make a minimum bet and play the hand crazily. I may stand on soft 17, which any floorman knows is an amateur move. Or I may hit a hard 14 against a dealer's stiff card, another bad play. All of these moves generally send a floorman away, annoyed that the dealer bothered him. But I only make these crazy plans if I don't want to leave the table because I've been constantly winning.

5 • Sometimes if a dealer is really co-operative, he or she may go out of his or her way to help you in a way you would never dare to ask for. I've had dealers just pass by my request to get a hit when they had a hard 16, with the 6 in the hole. I've had dealers pay me off continually on ties.

I've even had a dealer tell me what his hole card was. This was at a crowded table. I don't know why he did this. He'd just stare at me and say "four" or "nine," or whatever his hole card was. I'd toke him but I never would ask a dealer to do this for me. That's going over the line. But if they do it voluntarily, I'll take the information.

Sometimes a dealer is angry at the casino he's working for, or at a floorman or a pit boss. Or just angry. And you come along and treat him decently, and he decides to reward you. It happens occasionally. It always amazes me when it happens, for it comes at the most unexpected times. In those situations, I just keep toking steadily.

Let's now move on to the most important skill you must have to be a winner at gambling—money management. This next chapter is very important, so be sure to read it carefully.

15

MONEY MANAGEMENT

INTRODUCTION

Money management can be defined as making the best use of your bankroll for blackjack playing purposes. Your first goal is to improve and enhance the bankroll, making it bigger. The second goal is to preserve it in those situations where you've lost money at a table.

BLACKJACK'S ROLLER COASTER RIDES

Expect the unexpected when you play this game. You might sit down and have everything go your way and make a monster win one day, then play the next day and lose a considerable portion of the previous day's win. The game runs like that. Wins, losses, big wins, big losses, small wins, big losses, big wins, small losses, all in no predictable pattern.

Anyone who tells you they always win at blackjack isn't telling the truth. It's not a game where you can be sure of a win just because the game might be right and the rules perfect. After all, there's an element of luck in the game.

If you don't get the cards, you can't win. If you get the cards, you'll win.

But luck isn't the prime factor. Skill remains the dominant force. Playing correct basic strategy prevents you from making stupid plays which will eventually cost you money. Counting cards enables you to make the correct bets that will enable you to maximize your wins at the right times. Together, correct basic strategy, counting cards and altering your bets according to the count will make you a winner in the long run.

So, even if you encounter a losing streak, don't get discouraged. This happens to all good players, in fact, to all great players. It's just one of those things—the rules of blackjack cause these streaks and bad runs. But at the same time, these same rules, when taken advantage of, will make you a long-term winner.

YOUR WINNING EXPECTATION

Theoretically, with correct basic strategy, with correct counting and altering of bets, you should win 1 1/2 times your neutral bet per hour of play in the long run. Thus, if you're at a $5 table and your neutral bet is $10, you should average $15 an hour. At a $25 table, with a $50 neutral bet, your win expectation will be $75 an hour. A $100 neutral bet adds up to $150 an hour. And so forth.

But it doesn't guarantee that you'll win in the next hour of play or next five hours of play.

You may lose $200 one session, win $85, lose $150, win $35, lose $20, win $150, lose $55, lose $100, win $180, win $260 and end up winning $185 after all that effort.

You should win in the long run. What that long run is—it all adds up to the law of large numbers—is that the longer the sequence of events, the more the events will add up to their theoretical result. So, the more you play, the closer you'll get to the 1 1/2 times your neutral bet per hour win. Since you're not going to play millions of hours, your win expectation will equal the theoretical, plus or minus 20% or so.

For example, let's assume you've mastered the game, and feel comfortable with your bankroll at the $25 table, betting $50 as your neutral bet. If you play 100 hours of blackjack, your win expectation is $7,500, give or take 20%. Thus your win can be as high as $9,000 or as low as $6,000.

Or it can be lower than $6,000 or higher than $9,000, because 100 hours is the short run as far is this game is concerned. At the end of 1,000 hours of play, you'll be closer to the theoretical norm of $75 per hour profit than you'll be after 100 hours, and after 10,000 hours you'll be closer still.

So be patient when playing blackjack. Because of the rules, with the dealer acting last, and thus winning any hand where he busts, but you bust first, he is expected theoretically to win 47 our of every 100 hands. You'll win 43 of them and there'll be 10 pushes.

THE PLAYER'S ADVANTAGE

Well, you might ask, if you can't even win 50% of the hands you play, how can you end up a winner? The answer is in the player's, that is, your options. You get 3-2 for blackjack. You can double down at your option. You can split cards that are pairs. You can take insurance. Sometimes you can resplit pairs, sometimes you can double down after splitting pair. Sometimes you can surrender.

That's why mastering basic strategy is of utmost importance. All the options you can use are to your benefit. All should be used when the time is appropriate. Players who are ignorant of their options, or don't take advantage of them are just throwing money down the toilet. When you're at the blackjack table, be sure to find out just what options are available, and then use them all.

YOUR BANKROLL

Most of you, the readers, will be going to a casino for either a day or a week, or maybe longer, and you'll be able to play blackjack during that period of time. Therefore, you should be aware of two bankrolls; first, the overall amount of money you'll be taking with you for **extended playing**, and the **short term bankroll** necessary for any game you enter. That is, for any single session of play at one table.

OVERALL BANKROLL

Before you know how much money you're taking with you, you should know just what level of game you're going to be playing at. If you're going to be playing at a $25 table, then you'll need so much money. If you're going to be playing at a $5 table, obviously, you'll need less money.

Conversely, if your bankroll is limited for gambling, then you'll have to figure out what game will accommodate your bankroll. For example, if you're taking $500 to Vegas for a weekend, you would be foolish to be betting $100 a hand, or even $50 a hand. You'd be in danger of losing it all in one hour of bad luck.

1. OVERALL BANKROLL: MINIMUM & MAXIMUM STAKES

If you're going to be spending at least a weekend of play, or if you're going to a resort like Atlantic City and expect to put in a good eight to ten hours of blackjack, then you'll need at least 200-300 times your minimum bet as your bankroll for the time you're at the resort.

Thus, if you're going to be playing at a $5 table, the minimum you should take with you is $1,000 and the maximum you'll probably need is $1,500. $1,000 is perhaps scraping the bottom of the barrel—$1,500 would be a better sum to start with.

If you're at a $25 table, then $5,000 would be a minimum sum to have with you, and $7,500 a very comfortable sum to gamble with.

A $2 table would require $400-$600 for overall play, and at the other end, a $100 table would necessitate $20,000 to $30,000 as your bankroll.

Overall Bankroll Chart - Extended Play		
200-300 Times Minimum Bet Recommended		
Minimum Bet	**200x**	**300x**
$2	$400	$600
$5	$1,000	$1,500
$25	$5,000	$7,500
$100	$20,000	$30,000

These numbers may sound large to you—and you wouldn't want to lose all that money playing blackjack. We're not saying you're going to lose it all—it's just having a decent bankroll available so that you're not playing with scared money, that is, money you can't afford to lose without it tapping you out.

I can recall a number of times when I started playing blackjack in Vegas where I went down the drain for two days before the tide turned. If I didn't have my reserve, I would have been in Tap City and stopped playing. But I rode the crest of the bad tide and came back strong, winning each time.

We expect you to win as well, or if you lose, to lose a sensible amount without going overboard. But it's nice to know the reserves are there, just in case. As you shall see, in our section of losses at any one session, we're going to show you a sane formula for preserving your money even if the table is horrible.

2. SINGLE SESSION PLAY: STAKE NEEDED

A good plan is to have 50 times the minimum bet at the table for any single session of play. This means $250 for a $5 table, or $1,250 for a $25 table. If you want to stretch down to the minimum absolutely, go with $200 or $1,000 respectively, 40 times the minimum bet, but we wouldn't suggest figures lower than that.

These amounts of cash give you some leeway in the game and allow you to ride past losing streaks and still retain enough money to bounce back.

Sometimes, all it takes is a win or two and you've gotten back all your losses. An example might be this: You're at a $25 table single deck, and you're down $400. The deck is super-favorable, and since you're losing, you're drawing no casino heat or even interest by the floorman, who's watching a $100 table where some lout who doesn't know the first thing about the game is getting unconscious cards and winning several thousand bucks.

You bet $150, and get a pair of 9s. The dealer shows a 6. You now split the 9s and get another 9 and suddenly you have $450 out on the table, playing all three 9s as separate hands against the dealer's 6. You get an ace, 10 and 10 respectively on the 9s, and the dealer turns over his hole card, which is a 10. He holds 10-6, hits it, and gets a 7 and busts. You're now up $50.

If you were down $400 and only had taken $500 to the table, you could have bet only $100. If you didn't have any money in your pocket and no credit at the casino, you'd have had to stand with the 9s. You'd end up winning one bet.

You can take cash out of your pocket if you run out of chips and bet the cash as well. In the above example, if you had bet $100 and still had cash in your pocket, you could have split and resplit the 9s, but still your win would be less than with the chips on the table.

Be well-capitalized. You never know when the tide will turn in your favor, or when a succession of favorable runs will occur. You want to be ready for them and not impotently have them slip by. 50 times the minimum bet for a single session of play. It's an easy number to remember. Don't forget it.

Single Session Bankroll Chart
40-50 Times Minimum Bet Recommended

Minimum Bet	40x	50x
$2	$80	$100
$5	$200	$250
$25	$1,000	$1,250
$100	$4,000	$5,000

WINNING AND LOSING LIMITS: SINGLE SESSION

A. LOSS LIMIT STRATEGY

Here, we'll talk about the bad news first. What amount should you lose at any single session of 21?

1. LIMIT YOUR LOSSES

The first rule is this—never reach into your pocket after a loss, if you've used up all your chips, or if you need the cash to make a bigger bet than the chips you have on the table. In other words, limit your losses.

Once you reach into your pocket, once you start cashing traveler's checks, borrow money or cash a check for additional funds after losing your original table stake, you're courting disaster. *The first loss is the cheapest.* That's one of my favorite sayings. And one that will preserve your bankroll.

Never, never go after more money once the bankroll on the table is gone. Your session is over. Leave the table, get a snack, a soft drink, go back to your room and relax. Buy a paper or magazine or read a book. But stop playing blackjack for awhile.

2. QUIT IF YOU'VE LOST YOUR CONFIDENCE

The second rule is this—if you feel your money draining away at the table, and you feel unlucky, stop playing before you use up all the chips on the table. If you've lost confidence in the game, for whatever reason, get up and fly away.

Suppose nothing is going right. Your original $1,250 is now down to $600, but every time you double down, it's a disaster. No matter what card the dealer shows, be it an ace or a 6, you cringe. You feel you're beaten already. You have two 10s and have no confidence in your 20. Stop playing. Leave. You've dropped $650. That can be made up easily. $1,250 is a little tougher to make up. And you know in your heart you're going to be down everything if you continue playing. Time to leave.

3. STOP WHEN YOU'RE TIRED

The third rule is this—you've been losing, get nearly even, start losing again, and time is dribbling by. An hour and a quarter of playing and all you have to show for it is a bad headache and about $300 in losses. Not a huge loss, but you're sick of the game and tired. Get out and leave. Rest up and come back strong at another session.

4. STOP WHEN YOU'VE RECOUPED LOSSES

Rule number 4 is—you've been playing for a long time. So long you don't even remember if you've been at the table for one or two hours. Or you've switched tables a couple of times, losing at each one. Your original $1,250 has melted away to $475. And suddenly, at a new table, the cards turn. You get a couple of blackjacks. The deck gets very favorable and your double down wins. You win again by splitting 8s against a dealer's 10 and come up roses. Now, counting your chips, you find you're ahead by exactly $5.

What do you do?

Leave.

Anytime you've been behind and found yourself clawing your way back to even, or nearly even, get up and go. You've done well. By nearly even, suppose in the previous example, instead of being even, you find you're still behind by $15. Hey, that's nothing. Leave.

The worst mistake I see players make in any game is

this—they're way behind and they fight back to even or nearly even, then instead of leaving, they stubbornly stay on, and watch it all go down the drain again.

It's probably happened to you if you've played serious blackjack. You've been down $500 and find yourself down $20, but instead of leaving, you go on and finally quit when you've lost enough money to once more be down $500. At that point, how sweet it would be to only be losing $20. You regret not leaving the table at that point. It gnaws at your insides—you can't enjoy dinner. You have a sleepless night. You curse yourself for being stupid. Avoid all this grief. Leave when you're nearly even after a big loss.

Well, that's the bad news. Now, the good tidings.

B. MAXIMIZE WINNING STRATEGY

If you're winning, here are the rules to follow:

1. LEAVE A WINNER

If you're ahead substantially, you must think of leaving the table as a winner. Another terrible thing to do is to be ahead by $1,000 and end up losing. All that money down the drain. You can rationalize, and often players do, saying they only gave back the casino's money, not theirs. Oh, is that so? You mean that the chips in front of you aren't yours? That when you cash them in, the cashier at the cage says, "hey, that's the casino's money. Give it back."

Of course not. It's your money, not the casino's. If you're winning, leave a winner. Here's how you do that.

MONEY MANAGEMENT

a. The Stop-Loss Method:

This method is known to most stock-market investors or players. If they have a stock that's run up in value and they want to preserve the profits, they put in a stop-loss order. For example, they bought a stock at $20. It's now moved up to $34, but it's been hanging around that price, unable to penetrate it. It might go higher, but then again, it might drop in value. So the investor tells his broker he wants a stop-loss at 32. If the stock hits 32, it's automatically sold out. This way, he's preserved a 12 point profit. Or he might put in the stock-loss at 30, giving the stock a little more leeway.

And that's what we're suggesting you do with your winnings. You're ahead $1,000 at a $25 table. You've had a terrific run. Two dealers couldn't stop you. A third now enters the arena. Maybe things will still go your way. Or maybe they won't. It's impossible to know. Mentally, decide to leave with a profit of $800. You can move chips over, so that there's a distinct pile of $200. Once that's gone, you're gone. You know at that moment that you're going to win at least $800. That's not a bad feeling. It's a relaxing feeling. You're doing the right thing. You're acting intelligently, not stupidly.

But what if you continue winning? Now you're ahead $1,300. Keep a pile of $250 to one side. Now, you've guaranteed yourself a profit of $1,050. If you keep increasing your stop-loss, you've increase the amount of money you've guaranteed yourself in profits.

However, once you reach that stack and it disappears signifying the stop-loss has been reached, you're out of there. Gone. With a good profit.

187

Keep this in mind though. You may have to leave earlier if you detect casino heat, if a floorman is now scrutinizing your play. If the casino game is a good one and you want to play there again, get up and leave. Do this so it looks as if you have an engagement somewhere. Look at your watch. "Time for dinner," you might say. Or whatever. Chances are the floorman will offer you a comp for the meal. If he doesn't, don't ask. Just leave.

A stop-loss is good if you've won enough money. For example, if you're ahead $100 in a $25 game or $20 in a $5 game, there's no use in starting a stop-loss. But once you're ahead $500 or more, it may be time to do this.

2. HIT AND RUN WINS

If you're winning slightly, but have played for close to an hour, it may be time to leave, to avoid casino scrutiny and heat. My belief in blackjack is—hit and run. Win at one session, play again later on, preferably at another shift, where all the dealers and floormen are new.

3. CHAT UP THE FLOORMAN
WHEN WINNING

If a floorman comes along while you're winning, and winning substantially, it's always wise to engage him in conversation. Admit that you're ahead. Tell him that finally your luck has changed for the better. You can mention play at another shift, where you were buried the night before. He has no way of verifying this. It's the glum card-counters who look at every floorman as an enemy who get barred. Be friendly.

Ask about the food in the joint. He'll probably comp you and whoever you're with to a free meal, or maybe a show.

4. DON'T RATHOLE CHIPS

Never rathole chips. By **rathole**, we mean taking chips off the table and pocketing them during a session. Don't do this. It's a signal to the floorman or dealer that you're disguising the fact you're a winner. An ordinary player who wins is thrilled. A card-counter is thinking of heat and trying to minimize the win. Exult in the win, the way the ordinary players do. It'll minimize casino heat.

5. PLAY ONLY WHEN CONFIDENT

The same rules that apply to being tired or feeling no confidence apply to winning as well as losing. If you're ahead but real tired, or if you suddenly have lost confidence in your play or the cards, or whatever, get up and go.

Following these rules will end up enhancing your bankroll. You'll find yourself winning more and retaining your winnings and constantly building up your bankroll.

16

MAXIMIZING YOUR PROFITS

PLAY WITH THE STANDARD CHIPS OF THE TABLE

We have suggested a neutral bet of two units of the minimum bet allowed at the table you're playing at. Thus, if you're at a $5 table, the neutral bet will be $10. At a $25 table, it will be $50 and at a $100 table, it will be $200. For those playing at a $2 table, it will be $4.

That's easy enough. The neutral bet allows you to increase the bet fourfold from the neutral point rather than from the minimum point without getting much casino heat. Thus, if you're at a $5 table and start with $10 wagers, you may easily move to a $40 bet when the deck is super-rich for you without drawing too much attention.

If that kind of wager does draw attention, you can scale back to a maximum $30 wager without too much trouble. It depends on the attitude of the casino and the dealer and floorman.

What you basically want to do is bet with the same kinds of chips. If you're betting **nickels**, that is, $5 chips, discourage the dealer from paying you off in $25 chips. Otherwise, something like this might happen. You don't have many $5 chips let, and all you have now is a pile of $25 chips. You make a $40 bet using one $25 chip and three **redbirds**.

The dealer searches out the floorman and says in a loud voice, "green plays." What he is telling the floorman is that, though you're at a $5 table, you've increased your bets into the $25 range. Now the floorman may come over and pay attention to your game. Who needs this?

So, our first rule is: At whatever table you're at, play with the standard chips of that table. When you cash in originally, let's say at a $25 table, get all $25 chips. Don't ask for or take $100 chips. As long as you play these standard value chips, the chances of heat is minimal.

If a dealer is stubborn and keeps paying you off in higher denomination chips, keep changing color back to lower value chips. **Changing color** is changing the denomination of the chips.

INCREASE THE NEUTRAL BET
WHEN WINNING

We've spoken about the neutral bet and moving it up as the deck gets favorable for you. If you find yourself on a winning streak, increase the size of your neutral bet before the first round of the next deal. As we have often mentioned, blackjack is a roller coaster ride of riches and losses, of highs and lows, often without any discernible pattern. When you're on a roll, or a **rush**, as the pros say, take full advantage of it.

Let's assume you're at a $25 table. Your neutral bet

is $50, and you have increased it up to $200 in favorable situations without any heat, or even a second glance from the dealer. You are on a nice winning streak. After fifteen minutes, you're ahead $550. Now start with a $75 neutral bet. If you keep winning, make your neutral bet $100, then $125, then keep increasing it by $25 increments. While you're winning, you can make a really big score this way. Let's say the tide turns. How do you know? You lose two hands in a row.

Start again with $50, and now go into the stop-loss mode explained previously, where you're guaranteeing yourself a sure win of so much in chips set aside. If you continue losing, and get to the point where the stop-loss kicks in, get up and leave the game.

I coached a player to do this, and watched him play at a single deck game, where, although he started as a $50 neutral bettor, by the end of the session, he was making $300 neutral wagers. The cards were all coming his way. He ended up winning several thousand dollars, I believe $6,800, a monster win for a $25 table. The casino comped him to a room, meals, show, everything. They didn't even give him heat. He was betting big and winning big. He wasn't increasing his bet from $50 to $300, but from $300 to $800. That was reasonable as far as the casino was concerned.

Once you're betting above the neutral limit, what do you do when the deck turns negative? Let's assume you've worked your way from a neutral $50 wager to one of $150. The next round is negative. Drop it more than half. Move it down to $50. The chances are that the deck moves in one direction. It doesn't swing from positive to negative one round into the other.

If it does go positive, remember this. After winning a hand, it's natural for many players to **press their bet**, that is, put their winning bet on top of their original bet and try for a double score. Suppose a player has bet $100, and wins. A natural move is to press to $200.

You can follow this pattern. If you've reduced your wager because the deck is negative and then it gets positive, you can press your bet without drawing attention. But if you've lost the previous bet, be careful. Increasing wagers after losing bets is only done by two groups — *card counters* and *steamers*. We already explained that a steamer is one who is losing and going crazy, trying to win back his losses fast. Unless you can give a good imitation of a steamer, don't imitate one. And certainly, if you're way ahead, there's no reason to steam.

Just don't get greedy. Your neutral bet is $150, the deck gets cold, you drop to $50. You lose the hand but the deck get favorable. Raise your bet to $75 at the most. It pays to stay in action this way and not worry about being barred. You're playing against a casino which is basically greedy. One thing they can easily spot is the same sort of greed. There are some times when you just have to do with a smaller bet than the deck or decks call for to keep in action.

> *If you've reduced your wager due to a negative deck and then it gets positive, you can press your bet without drawing attention.*

NEVER INCREASE THE NEUTRAL BET WHEN LOSING

There's a tendency to forget winning principles when losing, and in order to avoid this, you must exercise strict control of your emotions. Even the best of the pros can get tired after a few long sessions of losing, of going from one table to another in the same casino, and still be unable to break even. There may be a tendency at this point to make a couple of big bets, pull even and get out. But don't do this.

If you're discouraged and tired, the best thing to do is leave the game and stop playing. Relax and rest. There's always another table and another game. If you take a nap for a few hours, you won't wake to find the casino has been emptied of all tables—that only vultures are flying near the ceiling. The games go on non-stop, day and night. There's always action, so you can pull away and refresh yourself without losing anything. In fact, you'll be doing yourself a favor in this kind of losing situation.

I would never raise my neutral bet while losing, and I wouldn't lower it either. If you have no confidence in the cards, leave the table. Don't lower your neutral bet. Get away.

The neutral wager allows you the freedom to go up and down. A minimum bet as a neutral wager only allows you to go up when the deck is favorable, and stay the same when it is negative. And it may prevent you from really raising the bet when the deck is super-favorable, because going more than four units from your neutral bet may cause casino heat, especially in a single-deck game.

TRY TO PLAY HEAD-TO-HEAD WHENEVER POSSIBLE

There are a four good reasons to do this.

1. First of all, you won't be playing with poor players who take away good cards from you by inappropriate splitting of 10s and other weird moves. This way you can avoid getting steamed by some stupid move that costs you a winning hand.

2. Secondly, and more importantly, you get many more hands per hour in. Playing head-to-head with a dealer is playing three times as fast as with one or two other players at the table. And the more hands you play, the more you should win theoretically.

3. Thirdly, it gives you a chance to handle the dealer better. You can establish a rapport that makes him willing to help you out, even unconsciously. You are the friendly one there alone with him. There aren't two losers complaining and moaning about their lousy cards while they destroy any chance they have of winning with bad plays.

4. Finally, you will see more cards in any deck In many casinos, the dealers are instructed to deal only two rounds in a single-deck game with a full table, or a table almost full. Then three rounds with three or four players. But with only one player, often they are using their discretion. If you treat the dealer like a human being, if you toke him appropriately, and establish a rapport, he may penetrate that deck really deeply and give you some situations that you'd never get with other players at the table.

DON'T ALWAYS SIT THROUGH
A TERRIBLE DECK

I have a few moves that have saved me money and grief. One of them is to stay out of hands where I know the dealer is going to deal three more rounds of cards when the deck is terrible. Let's say I'm at a single deck table with two other players. It's a $25 table and my neutral bet on the first round was whisked away by the dealer as he turned up a blackjack. I had 20, another player had a blackjack that he didn't have a chance to insure because the dealer showed a 10 as his upcard. And the third player had an Ace-9.

Let's further assume that this dealer gives us good penetration for the money. He goes way down into the deck. And that's what I'm facing. Three more rounds of nothing but trouble coming up. Already the deck is -4 and three aces are out.

I ask where the men's room is, and leave the table. Or else I suddenly have trouble with an eye, and get up and take out a handkerchief and leave the table as I poke around the corner of my eye. I do something to avoid three rounds of a really negative deck.

TABLE HOPPING

Table hopping is going from table to table in a casino, either in the same pit, or if the casino is big enough, to another pit altogether. I knew a cheap pro who did this just to avoid tipping any dealer, which he considered a capital crime. But that's not a good reason—in fact, it's a terrible reason. Dealers will have no sympathy for you once you get the reputation of being a turkey. They'll go out of their way to harass and annoy you, and who can blame them, if your only motive is to stiff them.

> *If I don't feel confident about a table, I leave it. That is some of the best advice I can give you.*

I will change tables in a pit or in a casino if the table I'm at has cost me money, and I've lost confidence there. I remember playing at a downtown casino where a friend of mine took half my action. We each put in $600 for me to play at a $25 table. Well, nothing went right. I would win one hand then lose two hands. Everytime the deck was favorable and I had a big bet out, I'd lose. When I had a minimum bet with a super-negative deck, I'd get a blackjack. It was awful.

About halfway into our stake, I got up and moved to another table in the same pit. The same thing. I was down to $300 and made my final move, to a woman I had played against who was ok. Finally, my luck turned. I regained my confidence in the cards. When I felt I was even, I got up. Actually I was ahead about $18 from the remnants of odd blackjacks. And we got comped in the steak house—so it wasn't too bad.

But I wasn't stubborn about the situation. If I don't feel confident about a table, I leave it. Probably to the floorman, if he was watching me, I was table hopping. But I usually don't do it. And certainly, I don't do it to stiff a dealer.

IF POSSIBLE, DON'T BE THE
BIGGEST BETTOR AT THE TABLE

This is good advice, but you can't always follow it. You may find yourself at a table with people who are cautious and bet only one or two units and that's it. The problem here is that if you start moving your bets up as the count gets strong, it'll be you the casino bosses will be looking at. Therefore, try and sit at a table with big bettors. This isn't hard to do. I find that big bettors scare off other players, who are afraid of getting dirty looks from them if they make a bad or wrong play. But you needn't concern yourself about that—knowing Basic Strategy and counting, you'll be making all the right moves.

I like to sit at a $25 table if there's only one player betting several hundred bucks a hand. This way I can sit to his left and be dealt the last cards on the round and make the last plays. My $50 neutral bet won't even be looked at. The floorman is watching the big guy with his black ($100) chips. I can do what I want. Sometimes, in this situation, I really raise the limits of my bets. If the deck is super-favorable at a single deck game, I may get in there with eight or ten units. I do this because my bet is usually insignificant to the other player's and even if I match him once in a while, they're still watching him.

Of course, if I make a couple of monster bets and win, and eyes turn my way, I taper down my bets, and let the heat move back to the big player.

PLAYING MORE THAN ONE HAND

You're allowed to play more than one hand at a table, provided that there are two empty spots adjacent to each other. If there's a spot in front of you and a spot on either side that's vacant, you can play two hands at once. You can even play more than two hands. You can play three, or all the spots at a vacant table.

The rules of this vary from casino to casino and in a casino, from table to table. Most casinos will allow you to play two or more spots if you bet double the table minimum on each spot. For example, if you are at a $5 table, it'll cost you $10 in wagers per hand you play. If you play three or more hands at once, the casino will usually let you play for the same amount per hand.

Once you play two hands at once, even if another player comes along and wants to play one of those spots, he can't. It belongs to you. But if you play two hands, then switch to one and then switch back again, the dealer or floorman may insist that you give up one spot to a new player.

When playing two hands at one, you can only look at the cards in one hand and play that hand out before seeing what your other cards hold. Of course, that's when the cards are dealt face down. When they're face up, you can simply observe all the cards that have been dealt, but you must still play one hand at a time in the order in which they've been dealt.

> *When playing two hands at once, you can only look at the cards in one hand and play that hand out before seeing what your other cards hold.*

When cards are dealt face down, and the dealer shows an ace as his upcard and asks the players at the table if they want insurance, you can look at all of the hands that you were dealt.

Is it worthwhile playing two hands at once? Well, you'll win more money if the cards run good, or you'll lose more if the cards aren't good. That makes it a guessing game. There are times, however, when you might consider playing two or more hands at once, switching from the usual one hand you've been playing.

Let's assume that you want to deplete a bad deck fast. You're at a $5 table and have been winning, and now your neutral bet is $25. The deck turns sour right away, with 10s and aces leaving it. You and one other player are at the table You now play two hands at $10 a hand and try to run out the deck as soon as possible. Betting $20 in this way, reducing your bet from a flat $25, doesn't look as though you're really dropping your betting limits that fast.

Or conversely, the deck is super-favorable, with all the aces in the deck, and you're afraid you're getting one final round of dealing from this dealer. By playing two hands with big bets out on each, you're putting a lot of money on the table in a way that doesn't appear as though you're skyrocketing your bets. For example, you're at a $25 table, and have been able to bet six units, or $150 on one hand without drawing heat. Now, with the super-rich deck, you make two bets of $150 each. You have $300 out there and are getting more cards, cards that would ordinarily be shuffled up after one more round of play.

Our final advice.

If you can get a game that's head-to-head against a dealer, play one hand at a time. You'll have more control over the situation, and your job now is to get the dealer to penetrate more deeply into the deck to your advantage.

You then can occasionally play two hands, either in unfavorable or favorable situations, as discussed previously.

17

EIGHT RULES OF SELF-DISCIPLINE

INTRODUCTION

There are any number of players who have studied blackjack, who know basic strategy and can count cards, and yet they're losers. They can't win because they haven't disciplined themselves to win. They lose control at key moments. They play hunches. They see a favorable situation and instead of making a sane bet, they make some wild outlandish wager, risking everything on one hand. And losing it.

It has always been one of my precepts—when you enter a casino, you're not only fighting the casino but yourself as well. If you don't have your emotions under control, you can't beat the house. The odds are just too strongly against this happening.

So, let's follow these simple rules, and take control of our lives in a casino.

EIGHT SIMPLE RULES

1. Don't Play with Money You Can't Afford to Lose Either Financially or Emotionally.

If you're playing with either scared money or money you need for something else, some necessity such as rent, a car, or whatever, don't play blackjack. Only when you feel you can afford to lose whatever you're playing with, and walk away undamaged either financially or emotionally, should you consider playing 21 for money.

Note that we said financially or emotionally. You may be able to afford to play financially, but if a loss upsets you to the point where it kills your day or unbalances you, don't play. It isn't worth it.

However, if you feel comfortable playing on both levels, then this is the game for you. It's a game with luck, to be sure, but there's enough skill to turn the game in your favor. After reading this book and practicing the moves outlined, you should be a winner.

2. Set Aside Sufficient Capital for the Game.

Don't be undercapitalized, or you'll be desperate for the early win, to protect your bankroll. Feeling this way, you'll alter your game to try and make an early killing. That's the wrong approach. What you want to do is have sufficient capital to weather initial losses and bounce back.

3. Make Bets within the Framework of our System.

Just because a deck is favorable, doesn't mean that you're going to win the next hand. It simply means that the deck is in your favor, but there are no guarantees. So don't go crazy with a couple of bets that tap you out.

For example, let's assume the deck is +5, halfway down, a very favorable situation. But not a guaranteed situation by any means. Instead of betting six units, you bet twenty units, half of your stake. There's no heat, and you are dealt a 10-9 but before you can even do anything, the dealer peaks under his 10 and turns over a blackjack.

One loss. Now the deck is still +3 with less than half a deck to go, so you want to make up that loss, and bet the other twenty units you have left. You're dealt an Ace-7 and the dealer holds another 10. Now you're afraid to even hit the soft 18, which is correct play.

You want to protect the 20 units you have out. You stand pat, and the dealer turns over another 10. You've lost 40 units—let's say it was a $25 game—a loss of $1,000 in two plays. It's a devastating loss. If you had bet six units originally, and then another six, even if you hit the soft 18 and lost, that's 12 units, or $250. It's a tough loss, but not devastation.

4. Never Reach into Your Pocket after Losing Your Original Table Stake.

We dealt with this before, but it's worth repeating, over and over again. **The first loss is the cheapest**.

If you were at a $25 table and lost $1,000, and then blindly and stubbornly played on, you're headed for real big trouble. First of all, you may be out of control, and instead of making $50 neutral bets, you're betting $300 at a time to get back your original loss quickly. Suddenly you've lost another $1,000 and then another and another, and as you stagger up to your room, you find you're down $4,000. What have you done?! You have a blinding headache and have given up on playing blackjack.

Of course, this kind of guilty remorse only lasts for a little while, as all gamblers know, and so you plot to make up the $4,000 by making even bigger bets. You have a credit card and take a cash advance against it, and start betting bigger and bigger as you lose more and more. Now you're down $12,000.

At this point, the $1,000 loss doesn't seem to be much at all. It's an amount you could have made up even with $50 neutral bets if you had a couple of good runs. But $12,000? How are you going to make that up.

We show this horrible situation no to scare you but to show you how dangerous it is once you start reaching into your pocket after you've lost what you have on the table.

If you've dropped what you had on the table, get up and walk away. Be sane, not stupid.

5. If you Find Yourself Angry at the Dealer or Other Players, Get Up and Leave the Table.

I've been at tables where a hostile dealer went out of his way to hurt my game. I got up and left. I've been also at tables where I had a huge bet out, was ready to double down, and the idiot next to me started splitting his 10s, till he depleted them. I didn't double down, and the dealer made his stiff hand into a winner. I wanted to strangle the fool next to me, but what can you do? I was steaming, so automatically, my precepts kicked in.

Steaming? Leave the table. Which I did.

If you start steaming, you're going to alter your play. You're going to bet bigger than you should. You'll stop counting. You'll be acting strictly on emotions rather than reason, which is essential to winning at blackjack. Cool off. Leave the table. The hell with the bozo who split his 10s, or hit his hard 16 against the dealer's 6, busted, while the dealer got a 5 on his hard 16. Forget about him. Cool out somewhere.

6. If You Sit Down and Find the Rules are Bad, Don't Even Play One Hand.

Don't be stubborn, and play in a game where you're killed by the rules in force. Don't think that fate has brought you here anyway to make a killing—you're the one who's going to be murdered in the end, and not by fate, but by the rules which say you can only double down on 10 or 11. As soon as you realize the rules are terrible, you're gone.

7. If You Get Casino Heat, Don't be Stubborn. Leave.

Let's say you're playing head-to-head and doing nicely. Then a floorman comes over and watches your game. He's extremely hostile, and treats you as if you're some cockroach crawling in from the cold. He has the dealer shuffle up after every round. If he sees big cards out he lets the dealer penetrate the deck for a couple of more rounds.

Why are you still sitting there? Get up and take a walk and cash in your chips. Leave the casino.

8. Don't Play if You've had too Much to Drink, if You're Tired, or if You're Sick.

When you sit down to play, you should be at the top of your form. If you've had a few drinks with friends, your skill is going to be impaired. You won't think clearly. Worse, you may feel unnaturally lucky and start making big bets. The drinks are making you braver than you should really be.

Dealer shows an ace—and you hold two 3s. Well, you feel lucky. Split them with your big bet out. Another 3. Split that also. Now you have $300 out and you don't even know what the count is. Was there a count? Hmm, there are some cards already played. Think the count is +. Or is it -?

Anyway, I got this 10 on the first 3. Got a hunch. Stand. Next card. A 7 on the 3. Geez, that would have given me a 20. Can I change my mind? No? Mmm. I'll hit this sucker and get my 10 and show the dealer. What's this? A 6. What do I have, dealer? 16. MMM. Let's see. I got to hit it. Can't stay with all stiffs. A 10. Busted.

Well there's the third 3. Where'd that 3 come from? How come I have three of them? What is this anyway? Oh, I split the 3s and resplit them. Against a 10? I did? Well, gotta hit the third 3. Got a 4 for a 7. I can count. Got to hit it again. A 10. There you are. Got a 17. Dealer's got an 8 in the hole. I lose everything. Geez. What I need now is another drink.

If you start thinking like that, it's easier to go to the men's room and flush your money down the toilet and then go to the sink and pour cold water on your face. Or better still, just wash up and keep the money in your wallet.

The same holds true when you're tired, or have a bad cold, or feel out of sorts or feverish. Why are you playing 21? Why aren't you in bed, curled up under some warm blankets and relaxing, drinking some coffee or hot tea, or just some orange juice. Why are you sitting and sweating at the table, wanting to lose everything so you can get to bed?

Don't think like that. Go directly to bed. Cash in and get outta there.

18

TAKING CONTROL OF YOUR GAME

In this section, we're going to discuss all the factors that will enable you to maximize your profits and keep you in action despite the casino's scrutiny. It will cover everything from where to sit at the table to casino countermeasures and how to handle them.

YOUR PLACE AT THE BLACKJACK TABLE

First of all, if you're ready to play blackjack and find yourself at the pit in a casino, don't just rush into any empty seat you find available. Be discerning and careful. Follow these rules.

A. Don't Sit at a Crowded Table

If the table has four or more players, avoid it. This means single deck as well as multiple deck games. If all the tables are filled, then don't play at the casino. Try another one. If you can't find space at any casino, then don't play that night.

The goal of playing blackjack is not to get action or

pass the hours in aimless gambling. The goal is to win money. If you can't win money, don't play. Don't trust to luck. If you want pure luck, go to a roulette wheel, not the blackjack pit.

Pros in blackjack are much like pros in poker. If they can't find a good game, they don't play. Be a pro yourself and follow that simple solid rule.

B. Study the Game Before Sitting Down

Suppose you're at a single-deck game in downtown Las Vegas. There are only two players at the game, but you find that the dealer will not penetrate the deck. Only two rounds and the cards are reshuffled. Or three rounds at the most when a lot of aces and 10s have been dealt out. That's not the table for you. You need to see more than fifteen or twenty-two cards in a game like that. You want the dealer to go beyond the halfway mark in the deck, to give you a chance at some really powerful situations.

Or you may find that the deck varies in terms of penetration. Sometimes the dealer stops after two or three rounds; sometimes the dealer goes almost to the bottom of the deck. But, as you study the cards, you note that the dealer is counting cards also. When the deck remains favorable, she reshuffles fast. When the deck is unfavorable, she'll go way down into the deck. Who needs this? Move to another table.

If the same situation seems to prevail at all the tables, get out of there. But this usually won't be the case. Dealers have other things on their minds besides counting. They have to make correct payouts, cash out players, add up the card totals. They have their own onerous duties. Counting cards doesn't have to be part of their job.

If you find another table in the casino, where there are less than four players, sit down if it seems right to you, if the dealer goes beyond the halfway mark in deck penetration.

Best of all, find a table where you can play head-to-head with the dealer. As mentioned earlier in the book, even if such a table is available, be careful if you confront a dealer robot with his or her arms crossed. Bad body language. Probably it's an empty table because everyone has already fled after being destroyed.

However, this doesn't have to be the case. Many players prefer just what you want to avoid; a crowded table. Why? Well, they're in the casino to gamble—they're not skillful and they don't count cards. They don't really have a grasp of basic strategy. They make mistakes. At a crowded table in a lower limit game, such as $2 or $5, they have plenty of company. Other players make mistakes also.

That's why, when you sit down at a table that isn't crowded, you'll often find the third base seat empty. Weak players don't like to sit there. When they make a mistake, they feel they've hurt everybody at the table if the dealer makes his hand, when he should have busted. Even when they make the right play, the others at the table moan and groan and give the anchorman a dirty look.

I watched a game where the anchorman hit his hard 12 against the dealer's 2, and busted. The dealer turned over a 10, and hit his own hard 12 and got an 8, beating everyone at the table. The players all stared at the hapless anchorman, who mumbled "I'm sorry," and flushed, left the table soon after. Correct plays don't always guarantee wins—but the player didn't even know he had made the correct play.

Someone else took his place, a woman. A couple of hands later, she stood on an Ace-6 when the dealer held a 5. The dealer turned over a 10 for a hard 15, hit the hand and got a 4 and beat everyone, most of whom had stood with stiff totals against the dealer's 5. But no one even bawled out the anchorwoman or gave her a sidelong glance. She had made a horrible blunder, and probably caused the whole table to lose, but her fellow players probably would have done the same thing.

I was at a $25 table (where the players are generally not much better) and split 9s against a dealer's 8. The commotion that followed! The verbal moans and groans! The muttered "Geez, what's he doing?"

I got an ace on one 9 and busted the other for no gain-no loss. The dealer held an 18. At least I had a shot at two wins in this situation, rather than a push. But my fellow players didn't even split 9s against a dealer's 4 or 5. They liked the 18 total.

C. Don't Play with Bad Rules

If you sit down and find the rules are bad. Get up again and leave.

There's no rule that says you must play one hand before leaving. Even after you've exchanged cash for chips, pick up the chips and go, if you find that the rules are too restrictive. I sat down at a game in a Strip casino which was single deck, whereas all the others were multiple deck, then asked about the rules, just to be on the safe side. Doubling down only on 10s and 11s. I picked up my chips and was gone, heading directly to the cashier's cage. I didn't even want to play one hand—why be stupid even for one hand?

If the whole casino has lousy rules, get out of there. I wandered into a small casino in Reno, where the rules seemed like everyplace else. But I noticed that the layout printing didn't say "Insurance Pays 2-1" a fairly standard rule in practically all American casinos.

> *The best place for you to sit is the anchorman's or the seat directly before the anchorman's seat.*

"Don't you have insurance here?" I asked.

"No, sorry, sir," the young woman replied rather pleasantly. I was up and gone, pleasantly.

D. Look for the Best Game

Even if you find a game that isn't crowded, if the only place open is in the first or second baseman's seat, look for another game. The best place for you to sit is the anchorman's or the seat directly before the anchorman's seat.

In the later seats, you get that extra piece of information, because other players have to act on their hands before you act on yours. Thus, a + deck can quickly turn into a negative deck. Conversely, a negative deck can turn into a plus deck. With about seven or eight cards dealt before you have to act on yours, you may change your strategy. This extra knowledge has won me a lot of money, and sometimes saved me the grief of doubling down or splitting cards that were no longer profitable moves.

On the other hand, if the dealer is sloppy or uncertain, maybe the first base seat is ok. We discussed first basing, where the sloppy dealer reveals his hole card when dealing. If you come across this situation, by all means sit down. But don't be obvious, and if a floorman starts watching your action, stop first basing immediately.

DEALING WITH CASINO PERSONNEL

A. Assume a Friendly Tone When You Sit Down

A dour, serious expression first of all turns off the dealer and secondly, if you play well, gives a signal to the floorman that a card-counter is playing.

Therefore, relax, smile, make yourself comfortable, as if you're just a tourist having some fun.

B. Study the Name of the Dealer on the Tag She Wears

If her name is "Nancy" for example, I like to start off the session saying, "Hi, Nancy, how's it going?" If she's friendly, fine. Maybe an extra toke at the right time will get her to deal an extra round of cards. Even if she won't do this, a friendly dealer can be helpful, either consciously or unconsciously. If she sees you're willing to toke, maybe a slight gesture after she peeks at her hole card gives away it's relative value.

C. Study the Dealer's Moves and Gestures

Most players are so busy studying their card totals that they never pay attention to the dealer. I watch to see how she deals, how she shuffles, how she peeks. Any one of these things can give away some valuable information. I've been able to follow the progress of an ace-10 through a shuffle, all the way to the top. I cut the cards so the ace and 10 were in the top part of the deck, and I bet more than I usually did, knowing their position.

Watch how the dealer peeks at her cards. Does she raise the card more after a stiff shows its face to her? Does she quickly spot a 10? Just one piece of information at the right time can make you a lot of money, or conversely, save you the grief of a big loss.

After she peeks, watch how she puts her two cards together. Sometimes, information can be gleaned with this innocuous gesture. A dealer satisfied with his hand, knowing he has a 10 below for a 20 hard total, may place the cards carefully together, or leave them slightly apart. The latter move is more common. The dealer knows he won't have to hit his hand and will probably collect from all the players facing him, so he slides the bottom card, his hole card, to one side so he can quickly turn it over and show his 20 and get on with his collecting of the player's losing bets.

Or a dealer hungry for tokes may want you to win, so when he has a stiff total, he's in a hurry, his body language saying "hurry up, don't take a card, let me bust." If a dealer changes speed in dealing out cards as the players act or stand, see what this signifies.

Most of the time, you may not get anything out of a dealer's gestures or moves. But there's always the chance that he'll give away something at some point. Maybe he's distracted, maybe something's on his mind, maybe he just saw his girlfriend walking through the casino with another man. Maybe...who knows? But always be alert at the table.

D. Act as if You're Not Really Paying Full Attention

You want to create a persona that is sort of indifferent to the game. Of course, you're interested in your own hand and the dealer's but you don't really care that much about the other players' cards. You can pay some attention to them outwardly, because in the course of a game, players watch other players make their moves. That's natural curiosity. But don't look like a counting machine. Balance the count quickly as it occurs and then relax. Don't keep staring back and forth across the table. The floorman will spot that move.

When you know that the last round has been played, and you've stood pat with your hard 17, pay no more attention to the game. Look around the casino, lean back and relax. There's really no reason to pay attention to anything. You'll either win, push or lose your bet, and nothing you do will change that. And the dealer is going to shuffle up anyway. So why pay attention?

This relaxed attitude pays dividends. You'll avoid a lot of casino heat.

E. Engage the Floorman in Conversation

I like to start out by asking how the food is at the buffet or dining room. If I'm playing a $25 game, I'll automatically get a comp for myself and my party. I talk to him about other things as well. If he has a name tag with his hometown, I mention that I was in that state not long before. I'm giving the appearance of paying attention to him and not to the table and the other players. Usually, it works and he'll go away, sign a comp ticket and bring it back to wish me luck and leave.

If he isn't interested in my small talk and is really scrutinizing my game, I won't make a stupid losing move just to assuage him. I figure he's on to me, and it's time for me to leave the casino.

I may ask him where the men's room is and just get up and go there for ten minutes. I'll come back and if he's gone, I may continue playing. If he's still at my table or comes right over when I come back, I'll shake my head and tell him my stomach really hurts—does he get many complaints about the buffet in the hotel? After all, he's not comping me to the meal—so it's a free-wheeling bad-mouth on my part. The hell with him.

F. If Countermeasures are Ordered, Don't Linger at the Table

The following are the standard countermeasures in increasing order.

We'll start with the weakest.

STANDARD CASINO COUNTERMEASURES

1. The dealer shuffles up more often.
2. The dealer shuffles up after every round of play, if I change my bet.
3. The floorman informs me that I can't alter my bet.
4. The dealer shuffles up after every round whether or not I alter my bet.
5. The dealer doesn't even deal to me, but passes my by.
6. The floorman asks me to leave the table.
7. The floorman calls over a security guard while telling me this.
8. The floorman wants my full name and proof of identification.
9. I'm accompanied to the cashier's cage to make sure I'm paid off and out of there.

I usually get the message after 1 or 2, and get up on my own and leave. But just because number 8 is stronger than number 1 doesn't mean the countermeasures can't start with the floorman coming over with a security guard to tell me I'm barred from the casino.

If casino countermeasures start, don't let them get out of hand. You have rights, but they have the security guards and the power at that moment. Don't fight them. Don't argue or ask questions. Just leave. Co-operate to an extent.

To what extent? Well, I'd never give them my name or identification to prove who I am. I'm not under arrest and there's no way they're getting that. I stand firm. Usually, that's that. I can leave.

This doesn't mean I've encountered this situation every

time I've played. I rarely get any casino heat these days. I've gotten older and learned how to remain at a table like any other tourist. I don't make expert moves like doubling down on soft 19 against a dealer's 6 if it will bring heat. I try and act friendly. I appear relaxed. If you follow our suggestions, you shouldn't get heat either. But if you do, let it end at the earliest level and just get up and leave. Don't fight the casino.

19

BEATING THE CASINO

From time to time I've taken on private students. They would seek me out when I lived in Las Vegas, and sometimes they'd write to me after reading one of my gambling books. One student, whom I'll call Pete, really wanted to learn the game. He was willing to spend as much time as possible practicing and memorizing correct play and proper card counting. He visited me in Vegas some years ago, and I remember him calling me and inviting me to dinner at the Horseshoe Club. He was staying at a Strip hotel, but was playing at the Horseshoe because of their single deck game. Pete had taken a beating at the Horseshoe playing blackjack and was comped to their steak house, so he asked me to join him.

Pete was a little over normal height, I'd say about 5'10" with broad shoulders. He was a good-looking guy from New York, and told me that years ago he had fought in the Golden Gloves as a middleweight. He still looked in good shape though he was now a light-heavyweight, and someone I wouldn't want to get into the ring with. I guessed he was in his late thirties at the time.

He was waiting for me outside the restaurant, dressed

informally, but wearing a sports jacket and a thin gold chain around his neck. Clothes looked good on him. We shook hands and waited for the maitre d' to show us to a booth. He ordered a couple of imported beers for us, leaned back and looked me over.

"How'd you hear about me?" I asked. "Did you read one of my books."

"I'm not much for reading, to tell you the truth. Someone in Brooklyn told me to look you up. You know Sally Pops?"

It was a name from long ago, a connected guy who had been represented by my father, who had practiced law in Brooklyn. I nodded.

"Well, he heard I was going to Vegas and he said, 'look Ed up if you want to be a winner.' "

"That was nice of him," I said. "How's he doing?"

"Fair, just fair." Pete didn't elaborate and I didn't ask any more questions. The waiter came over with our beers and we ordered dinner. Both of us had shrimp cocktail and steaks. When the waiter left, we started talking about blackjack.

"How you doing?" I asked.

"Not too good. I try and get on a rush and then end up getting killed. What I do is double my bet after a win, sometimes triple it. I get a little rush going and then, boom, the goddamn cards go against me."

I nodded.

"I think I play a good game, but I don't know. I'm down a few grand already."

"What stakes are you playing?"

"I stick to the quarter table. I'll go up to $50 bucks

sometimes, but I bet more when I'm on a streak. A winning streak. When I lose a hand I go back to $25. So what do you think?"

The waiter brought us shrimp cocktails and another round of beers.

"Do you know the game cold?"

"I used to think so, but to tell the truth, I don't know anymore."

"Ok, Pete, you mind if I ask you a couple of questions?"

"Go ahead."

"You're dealt an Ace-6 and the dealer shows a 3. What do you do?"

"Hit."

"You're dealt a 7-3 for 10 and the dealer shows a Queen?"

"Double down."

"You have an Ace-6 and the dealer shows a 7?"

"Hit. How'm I doing?" Pete asked.

"The last one you got right. When you hold a soft 17 you're either going to hit it or double down, depending on the dealer's upcard. You should double down against the dealer's 2 through 6 with that soft 17."

He nodded.

"And you don't double down a 10 against a 10. If the dealer is holding a 20, all you can hope for is a push. And you're doubling your bet on a bad proposition."

He nodded, chewing on a shrimp.

"What you want to do is master basic strategy, and then learn a counting system. Do you know about counting?"

"Yeah, somewhat. If the aces are out of the deck it's no good for you. The same with the 10s."

"Well, 10s are going to constantly come up in the course of a game. You want to count them in relation to the small cards, 3 through 6s."

He was willing to learn, and I told him it would take several hours, or maybe less. Pete was in for the weekend, and this was already Friday night. I knew he was dying to get back to the tables, but I told him to be patient. We left the Horseshoe and I drove back to my apartment, near UNLV. I made some coffee and cleared a table, took out a deck of cards and started dealing hands.

"What I want you to do is be patient," I said. "I'll deal to you until you have things pat. You already know some of the correct moves and I can tell you want to play aggressively, so that's in your favor."

"How long will it take?"

"As long as it takes. I'll tell you when you're ready. You have to be patient, Pete. I had a guy from Hollywood visit me a couple of months ago. He's a producer. Small-time. We practiced for about an hour, and he got bored. He knew it all, he told me, though I could see he was still making mistakes and didn't know how to count cards. So he went out and lost everything.

"You've got to remember, Pete, the casinos make a fortune from blackjack. They stack the rules in their favor. But the game can be beaten. It takes knowledge and self-discipline."

"And luck..."

"Luck is going to even itself out in the long run."

"I won't be here in town for the long run."

"No, but you'll be here long enough. Shall we begin?"

I dealt out cards at random and asked him what moves he'd make. Then I changed the format by dealing specific hands to specific dealer cards. For example, I put out the deuce as the as the dealer's upcard, and showed an Ace-2 and all subsequent soft hands and asked Pete what he'd do in each instance; that is, stand, hit or double down. From soft hands I switched to hard totals. Then I did the same thing with a 3 upcard, and the 4 upcard, all the way to the dealer's 10-value and Ace upcards.

In this way, I went through every possible combination, except for pairs. It took him a couple of hours to get the correct feel of the game. Pete was fortunate, in that numbers came easily to him. He told me that he had an uncle who was a bookmaker in New Jersey and he'd help him out during the football season. He was at home with numbers and odds.

We next concentrated on pairs. Which did we split and which didn't we split?

We took a break here, and I drove him back to his hotel. Then, the next morning, I picked him up and took him out for breakfast, and back to my place. We reviewed what had been gone over the night before, then worked the pairs. I showed him the rationale behind the decisions; for example, we split 9s against an 8 because all we have is a potential tie, whereas we stand with the 9s against a dealer's 7 because we have a potential win.

Next I showed him how to count, using a simple system, balancing the 3s through 6s with 10-value cards, and keeping a separate count of the Aces. When more

Aces than normal were in the deck, he was to bet more, especially with a plus, or favorable count. Then I started dealing cards, using a random deck, and he made bets from two units (neutral) down to one (minus) and up to four, five or six (plus values).

"When we had dinner the other night, you told me you automatically doubled up after every win..."

"And got my clock cleaned..."

"That's because whether you win or lose a hand has no bearing on the next hand you play. What is important is the count, showing you whether the deck is favorable, neutral or unfavorable. Now here's the thing. It's unusual for a non-counter to lower his bet after a win, so don't do it. And it's usual to raise a bet after a win. If the deck is favorable, triple your bet. They won't care. But don't do that after a losing hand. You'll draw heat. So, let's say you win the first hand and the deck is minus. Keep the same bet out there. If the deck is favorable add a couple of units to your bet. If the deck is neutral, add one unit. You like to play aggressively and I don't want to cramp your style.

"And if I lose the first hand and the deck is minus?"

"Then bet the minimum. That's ok with the floor-man."

We practiced counting and playing and betting according to the count, changing not only betting strategies but playing strategies as the count changed. We broke for lunch and Pete went back to his hotel for a nap. I met him that evening at the Horseshoe, and he went to a $25 minimum table while I stood a bit back from him. There were two other players at the table. Pete followed my instructions exactly, taking a grand from the dealer in quarter chips and starting out by betting two.

The dealer was hot and before a half-hour passed, Pete was down $500, then in a little while he had $200 left. With a new dealer, he clawed his way up to $600. Then he went bad again, and left the table with $400.

We took a walk to let him cool off.

"I feel confident," Pete said, "I can beat the game. I just had a run of bad luck."

We went back to the Horseshoe and Pete cashed in another grand at a $25 table. He won a few hands and after a half-hour was up about $300. At the next table, a young dealer stood with his arms crossed. In front of him was an empty table with a sign reading "$100 minimum." Pete got up and sat at the table, handing his chips to the dealer. "Change color," he told the dealer.

He was given thirteen $100 checks. Pete stacked and restacked them and then put out two. The dealer shuffled up the cards, burned one and dealt Pete a blackjack. Pete left three checks on the table and won the next hand. And so it went. Pete was ahead almost five thousand when another man sat at the table, a beefy guy with a red face, who asked for a marker for $5,000.

"How's it going?" he asked Pete.

"I'm almost even. Last night I dropped close to six grand." That was for the floorman's ears. I had rehearsed this type of response in my apartment. You've always lost the night before or at a different shift. That was the line.

"You play here?"

"Yeah. I like the steaks here. Maybe this floor guy will comp me."

The floorman, who had been standing nearby, sprang

to attention.

"What's your name, sir?" Pete gave him a name.

"Are you staying here?"

"No. Make that comp for two. My friend here is hungry."

The floorman looked me over. I guess I looked somewhat familiar but I saw he couldn't really place me. He handed the comp to Pete.

The other player was terrible; a degenerate gambler, betting on hunches. Once, with the deck as bad as it could be for the players, he put down $1500 and stood on a 16 against the dealer's 5. The dealer turned over a 3, got another 3 and then a 6 for a 17. The guy signed another five-grand marker. Pete, meanwhile was winning more. The floorman, to test him, had the dealer shuffle up after Pete had won a $600 bet. Following my previous instructions Pete kept the bet intact and won again.

By the time we packed it in for dinner, Pete had cashed in $12,000 in profits. We went to the steakhouse and had a leisurely steak dinner.

"How'm I doing?" Pete asked.

"Doing real well."

"I feel good. I'm going to play a grand a hand next. I got close to twenty grand. I'm going to bury them."

"Pete, anything can happen in the short run."

"No kidding. That's why I'm going to take a shot."

We took another walk after dinner, then were back at the Horseshoe. It was a bit after ten in the evening. The beefy guy was no longer around. Pete spoke to a floorman. He wanted a $1,000 minimum table to himself. No problem.

After the sign was put up, a crowd gathered behind Pete. He winked at me, then put out $20,000 in bills. A floorman plus the pitboss was behind the dealer. This time it was an Asian woman, who brusquely shuffled up. Pete put out two chips. $2,000. He was going to bet as though these were $25 checks. Start off with two, go up to four or five and down to one depending on the count.

"How you doing?" Pete asked the dealer.

She didn't respond and she didn't even smile. All business.

Pete picked up his cards. He held an 8 and 7. The dealer showed a King. Pete hit, got a Queen and busted. The dealer had a 10 in the hole. Pete reduced his bet to one check and managed a push with a hard 18. He got another push on the next hand, with a hard 17. Still betting one check, he lost the next hand, 19 to 20. The deck was pretty bad, and he lost another check, then pushed. The dealer reshuffled. So far it had cost Pete $4,000. He hadn't even come close to winning.

With the new deck, Pete bet two checks. The dealer got a blackjack, then a 20, then Pete finally won. But already three Aces were out of the deck, and he bet just one check. He lost that one, pushed, lost, pushed. $4,000 more lost. The dealer reshuffled again.

With $8,000 left, Pete bet two checks on the new deck. He lost, with a 17 against the dealer's 18. Betting one check, he pushed. He pushed again, then lost. Then lost again. The dealer wasn't reshuffling and Pete now had four checks left. He bet a check, and won, then lost a one-check bet. The woman reshuffled. She stood there, unsmiling, erect, her hands flying around the cards. Pete played with the four checks, then after she burned the top card, he put out two checks and lost, his 18 shorter than her 19. Two checks left, with the count at -2. He hesitated, and she waited, her hands high in the air holding the deck.

Finally Pete put out one check, and got 8s. The dealer showed a 10. The correct play here was to split the 8s. You always split 8s and Aces, to reduce your losses overall.

"Can I surrender?" Pete asked the dealer. She looked to the floorman. The floorman spoke up for her.

"We don't allow surrender."

So Pete split the 8s. He got a 5 on the first 8 and pointed at the cards for another hit. He was dealt a Jack and the dealer swept the cards and his check off the table. I could see a trace of a smile on her face. She was thinking, another loser in a city of losers. Pete took a deep breath and pointed at the other 8. He got a deuce.

"Big card," he said softly. He got a 7. Now he had to stand. The dealer turned her hole card over. It was a 4. She hit and busted with a 9. The cards were reshuffled. I looked around me. The crowd had thinned out, with only a few people still watching Pete play, while a security guard stood nearby.

New deck, new deal. The woman waited for Pete, who played with his two checks. Then he put both of them out. He got a 10 and 7 and the dealer showed a 5 as her upcard. Pete stood and the dealer turned over a 6.

"Jesus," said Pete softly.

The dealer separated the cards, then taking her time, dealt herself a 4 for a hard 15. Then a 7 and busted. The deck was plus 2, and Pete bet all four checks. He got 10, 9 and faced the dealer's 5. He stood and she turned over an 8 for a 13, then dealt herself a 4 for 17. Pete now had eight checks. The count was plus 3. She stood waiting for him to make a decision, and Pete put out all eight checks. The crowd had started to fill out again, and I could hear the buzz behind me. The dealer hesitated, then dealt out the cards. Pete got two tens, and the dealer showed an Ace.

"Insurance?" she asked softly.

Pete took a deep breath, then slowly shook his head. The dealer turned over the hole card. It was another Ace. She dealt herself a third Ace. Then a 10. She had a hard 13, and busted with a King. Pete now had sixteen checks. The dealer reshuffled. Pete cut the cards and the top one was burned. She waited for him to remove checks or stack them up but he said, "deal."

She moved to straighten out his checks but he said "leave them alone. You're bad luck." She turned toward the pit boss, who had been watching all the time. He nodded. She dealt the cards. Her upcard was an 8. Pete played with his closed cards the way a poker player would, shuffling them in his hands at random.

The dealer said "Only one hand. You can't hold them in two hands." Pete looked at her, his eyes cold, and turned over one of his cards. It was the Ace of spades.

"Snapper," he said, and then turned over the other card. It was the Jack of spades.

"Snapper it is." He waited while she paid off the bet. Twenty four more checks. He now had forty grand in front of him. This time he pulled the checks off the betting box and stood up.

"That's it," he said.

He stuffed the checks into his pocket, as the pitboss

came around to his side of the table.

"Would you like a room here? Comped?"

Pete shook his head.

"Any other place in town? We'll take you by limo."

"Nah." He looked at the dealer, who was waiting for him to give her a toke. For the first time, she was looking friendly. But Pete turned and went to the cashier's cage, and got packets of $10,000, four of them, and stuffed them into his pockets. Then he went over and gave the dealer a $100 bill.

On the way out, he said to me... "She wanted me to lose. Jesus, she wanted to bust me. Could you feel it?"

I nodded.

"But I had to toke her something. Good karma."

"Where'd you learn that?"

"Hey, I do a lot of reading. So, how'd your pupil do?"

"You did good. It was pretty tense for awhile."

"Yeah, that's how I like it."

"Well, you had the balls to keep raising with the plus deck."

"No lie."

He winked at me. "Come on, let's have some fun. The night's young and this money is burning a hole in my pocket."

Pete put one beefy arm around my shoulders as we left the casino. And off we went into the hot Vegas night.

20

FIVE PRACTICE QUIZZES

QUIZ NUMBER 1

You're at a downtown Las Vegas casino where you can play at a single-deck game. The rules are—dealer hits soft 17, doubling down on any two cards permitted. In the following instances, answer whether you hit, stand, double down or split pairs.

In all situations, you'll see the dealer's upcard.

Your Hand	Dealers's Upcard	Decision
1). Ace-6	7	_____
2). Ace-6	2	_____
3). Ace-2	3	_____
4). 10-6	6	_____
5). 9-9	8	_____
6). 9-9	7	_____
7). 2-2	2	_____
8). Ace-9	10	_____
9). Ace-5	5	_____
10). 6-3	7	_____
11). Ace-2-3	10	_____
12). 4-4	7	_____
13). 3-3	4	_____
14). 7-7	8	_____
15). 6-5	Ace	_____
16). 5-5	Ace	_____
17). Ace-7	9	_____
18). Ace-7	3	_____
19). Ace-4-2	8	_____
20). 10-3	2	_____
21). 10-2	2	_____
22). 10-3	6	_____
23). 8-8	Ace	_____
24). Ace-4	6	_____
25). 10-10	6	_____

ANSWERS TO QUIZ NO.1

1). Hit
2). Double down
3). Hit
4). Stand
5). Split
6). Stand
7). Hit
8). Stand
9). Double down
10). Hit
11). Hit
12). Hit
13). Split
14). Hit
15). Double Down
16). Hit
17). Hit
18). Double Down
19). Hit
20). Stand
21). Hit
22). Stand
23). Split
24). Double Down
25). Stand

QUIZ NO. 2

You're in Atlantic City, and look smartly for a four-deck, rather than a six-deck game. Other than the number of decks, all rules in all casinos are the same. The rules are doubling down on any two cards, dealer stands on all 17s, split pairs can be doubled down. There is no surrender. As in regular play, you'll see your cards and the dealer's upcard. Decide whether to stand, hit, double down or split pairs.

Your Hand	Dealer's Upcard	Decision
01). 10-2	3	_____
02). 8-8	9	_____
03). 3-3	2	_____
04). 9-9	7	_____
05). Ace-4-2	7	_____
06). Ace-8	5	_____
07). 5-5	Ace	_____
08). Ace-7	10	_____
09). Ace-7	Ace	_____
10). 4-4	4	_____
11). 6-6	2	_____
12). 10-6	7	_____
13). 4-4	6	_____
14). Ace-4	5	_____
15). Ace-2	3	_____
16). Ace-Ace	Ace	_____
17). Ace-6	2	_____
18). 9-4	3	_____
19). 3-2-Ace-Ace	9	_____
20). Ace-8	10	_____
21). 9-9	8	_____
22). 7-7	7	_____
23). 2-2	8	_____
24). 3-3	9	_____
25). Ace-6	6	_____

ANSWERS TO QUIZ NO. 2

1). Hit
2). Split
3). Split
4). Stand
5). Hit
6). Stand
7). Hit
8). Hit
9). Hit
10). Split
11). Split
12). Hit
13). Split
14). Double Down
15). Hit
16). Split
17). Hit
18). Stand
19). Hit
20). Stand
21). Split
22). Split
23). Hit
24). Hit
25). Double down

QUIZ NO. 3 - ADVANCED PLAY

You're playing single deck downtown Las Vegas with two other players. The dealer hits soft 17, You can double on any two cards. No surrender, no doubling after splitting. The deck is half depleted, and the count is +3. What's your play?

Your Hand	Dealer's Upcard	Decision
1). Ace-6	2	_____
2). Ace-2	4	_____
3). Ace-7	3	_____
4). 9-9	7	_____
5). 8-4	3	_____
6). 7-5 (Insurance?)	Ace	_____
7). 10-6	10	_____
8). Ace-7	2	_____
9). 5-5	3	_____
10). Ace-8	5	_____

The deck half-depleted, the count is -2. What's your play?

Your Hand	Dealer's Upcard	Decision
11). 10-2	4	_____
12). 10-2	3	_____
13). A-2	4	_____
14). 2-2	7	_____
15). 6-4	9	_____
16). Ace-6	3	_____
17). Ace-4	3	_____
18). 9-7	10	_____
19). 5-3	6	_____
20). 6-6	4	_____
21). 9-9	3	_____
22). Ace-7	4	_____
23). 9-4	2	_____
24). 5-5	8	_____
25). Ace-7	10	_____

ANSWERS TO QUIZ NO. 3

1). Double Down
2). Double Down
3). Double Down
4). Stand
5). Stand
6). Take insurance.
7). Stand
8). Double down
9). Double down
10). Double down
11). Hit
12). Hit
13). Hit
14). Split
15). Hit
16). Hit
17). Hit
18). Hit
19). Hit
20). Hit
21). Stand
22). Double Down
23). Hit
24). Double down
25). Hit

QUIZ NO. 4

You find yourself at a Strip casino in Vegas or a riverboat, playing a four-deck game. The rules here are: doubling down on any two cards, no surrender, no doubling down after splitting pairs, dealer stands on all 17s.

What do you do in the following situations?

Your Hand	Dealer's Upcard	Decision
1). 10-2	3	_____
2). 9-4	3	_____
3). Ace-5-Ace	7	_____
4). 2-2	2	_____
5). 3-3	3	_____
6). 4-4	6	_____
7). 8-8	Ace	_____
8). 6-6	2	_____
9). 9-9	10	_____
10). 9-9	Ace	_____
11). 6-5	9	_____
12). 8-3	10	_____
13). 6-3	7	_____
14). 5-3	6	_____
15). Ace-2	4	_____
16). Ace-5	10	_____
17). Ace-6	2	_____
18). Ace-6	3	_____
19). Ace-7	2	_____
20). Ace-Ace	Ace	_____
21). Ace-7	8	_____
22). Ace-7	10	_____
23). Ace-7	Ace	_____
24). Ace-4	4	_____
25). Ace-5	5	_____

ANSWERS TO QUIZ NO.4

1). Hit
2). Stand
3). Hit
4). Hit
5). Hit
6). Hit
7). Split
8). Hit
9). Stand
10). Stand
11). Double Down
12). Double Down
13). Hit
14). Hit
15). Hit
16). Hit
17). Hit
18). Double Down
19). Stand
20). Split
21). Stand
22). Hit
23). Hit
24). Double Down
25). Double Down

QUIZ NO. 5 - ADVANCED PLAY

You're at a Las Vegas multiple deck game using four decks. You've learned to count cards, and now have to make the following betting and playing decisions according to the count.

1). The Count is -1. How many units do you bet? _____

What is the correct move below based on this minus count?

Player's Holding	Dealer's Upcard	Decision
2). 13	3	_____
3). 7-7	10	_____
4). 6-3	4	_____
5). 10	9	_____
6). Ace-2	5	_____
7). Ace-3	6	_____
8). Ace-5	5	_____
9). Ace-7	3	_____
10). 3-3	5	_____
11). 6-6	3	_____
12). 9-9	3	_____

13). The count is +1. How many units do you bet? _____

What is the correct move below based on a +1 count?

Player's Holding	Dealer's Upcard	Decision
14). 5-3	6	_____
15). 6-3	10	_____
16). 8-3	Ace	_____
17). Ace-2	3	_____
18). Ace-2	4	_____
19). Ace-6	3	_____
20). Ace-7	8	_____
21). Ace-8	6	_____
22). Ace-3	3	_____
23). 2-2	3	_____
24). 9-9	7	_____
25). 6-6	2	_____

ANSWERS TO QUIZ NO. 5

1). One unit
2). Hit
3). Hit
4). Hit
5). Hit
6). Hit
7). Double down
8). Double down
9). Stand
10). Hit
11). Hit
12). Stand
13). Two units.
14). Double down.
15). Hit
16). Double down
17). Hit
18). Double down
19). Double down.
20). Stand
21). Double down.
22). Hit
23). Split
24). Stand
25). Split

21

GLOSSARY

A

Anchorman - See Third Baseman.

B

Barring a Player - The Casino's refusal to allow a player to participate in a blackjack game in its casino.

Blackjack -1. The name of the game. 2. The best holding in the game, consisting of an original hand containing an ace and a 10-value card

Break - **See Bust**.

Burn a Card - The dealer's removal of the top card in the deck after a shuffle, placing it out of play.

Bust - Having a hand totaling more than 21 points, which makes it an automatic loser.

C

Card Counter - A skillful player who keeps track of the cards as they are dealt out.

Card Counting - Keeping track of various cards as they are dealt out to determine if the deck is favorable or unfavorable to the player.

D

Dealer - The casino employee the player faces, who deals out cards, pays out winning bets and collects losing bets.

Deck - The standard 52-card pack of cards used in blackjack.

Double Down - The option a player has to double his bet on a particular hand and receive but one additional card to that hand.

Doubling Down After Splitting - An option available only in certain casinos where a player may double down after splitting a pair.

Draw A Card - See **Hit**

E

Early Surrender - The option a player has to forfeit half his bet and not play out his hand, before the dealer checks to see if he has a blackjack.

F

Favorable Deck - The cards remaining in the deck are in the player's favor.

First Baseman - The seat to the extreme left of the dealer; the first player to receive cards from the dealer

First Basing - The player in the first seat who is able to see the dealer's hole card.

Flat Bet - To bet the same amount each time without deviating.

Floorman - A casino supervisor who oversees a group of blackjack tables.

H

Hand - 1. The cards originally dealt to the player. 2. The final total held by the player after hitting.

Hard Total - Any hand where there is no ace, or where the ace counts as one.

Head-to-Head - Playing one on one with the dealer, without any other players at the table.

High Roller - A bettor who wagers big money.

Hit - The act of drawing a card to the original hand.

Hole Card - The dealer's unseen card, part of his original two-card holding.

House - Another term for the **Casino**.

I

Insurance, Insurance Bet - An optional bet that can be made by the player only when the dealer's upcard is an ace, which pays 2-1. The player is betting that the dealer has a blackjack.

Insure a Blackjack - A bet, usually unfavorable, made by a player who has a blackjack when the dealer shows an ace. It is paid off at even-money.

M

Marker - An IOU signed by a player who has casino credit.

Mucker, Hand Mucker - A cheat who adds favorable cards to a multiple deck game.

Multiple Deck Game - Any game of more than one deck, usually designating four or six deck games dealt from a shoe.

N

Natural - See **Blackjack**.

Nickels - Casino term for $5 chips.

P

Paint - A term signifying a jack, queen or king.

Pat Hand - An original holding of hard 17 or higher.

Penetration - The number of cards the dealer will deal out in either single or multiple deck games before shuffling up.

Pit Boss - A casino supervisory employee who is in charge of an entire blackjack pit.

Pit, Blackjack Pit - An area set aside in a casino to house a group of blackjack tables.

Push - A tie between a dealer and player, with no one winning or losing.

Q

Quarters - Casino term for $25 chips.

R

Redbirds - See **Nickels**.

Reshuffle - See **Shuffle Up**.

Round, Round of Play - A complete series of play in which all the players and the dealer act upon their hands.

S

Shoe - A box containing multiple decks of cards, designed so that the cards can easily be dealt out one at a time.

Shuffle, Shuffling Up - Mixing up the cards prior to a new deal.

Single Deck Game - A game in which only one deck of cards is used.

Snapper - A slang term for a blackjack.

Soft Hand, Soft Total - Any hand containing an ace which has a value of 11.

Splitting Pairs - The option of a player to split two identically ranked cards, such as 8s, and play each as a separate hand.

Stand, Stand Pat - The decision of a player not to draw a card to his original hand.

Stiff Card - A card ranked from 2 to 6, which may force the dealer to hit his hand.

Stiff Hand - Any hand totaling 12-16 which is in danger of busting if a 10 is dealt to it.

Surrender, Late Surrender - The option by a player to forfeit half his bet and not act upon his hand only after the dealer has checked to see that he has no blackjack.

T

Ten-Poor Deck - A deck in which more 10-value cards proportionally, than small cards have been dealt out previously.

Ten-Rich Deck - A deck in which more small cards proportionally than 10-value cards have been dealt out previously.

Ten-Value Card - Any card having a value of 10 points; a 10, jack, queen or king.

Third Baseman - The player in the last seat at the table, thus to the dealer's extreme right, who receives his cards and acts upon his hand last. Also called **Anchorman**.

Tip or Toke - A gratuity given to the dealer by the player.

Twenty-One - Another name for the game of Blackjack.

U

Unfavorable Deck - A deck whose remaining cards favor the casino rather than the player.

Unit - A standard bet size, usually in line with the chips issued by the casino.

Upcard - The dealer's exposed card, seen by all the players.

A

ADVANCED STRATEGY ORDERING

5 PROFESSIONAL REPORTS TO TURN AMATEUR CARD COUNTERS TO PROS

NOT FOR BEGINNERS—FOR CARD COUNTERS ONLY.

NEW AND REVISED! These **groundbreaking** reports have been relied upon by **professional blackjack players** for more than 25 years. And now, they are completely updated for today! This is a **big event** for winning and pro blackjack players.

THE LEGEND REVEALS HIS SECRETS - These professional strategies are the personal work of Arnold Snyder, **legendary** blackjack player and guru to thousands of serious players. Snyder, **one of the greatest players** in history and a member of the **Blackjack Hall of Fame**, is the author of nine books and advanced strategies including his national best-seller, *Blackbelt in Blackjack*.

THE PROFESSIONAL COUNTERS SECRET STRATEGIES - Start **winning** by applying the strongest betting strategy with the lowest risk. Good for all valid counting systems, some of the technical questions answered are:

- What's my advantage if the dealer deals out 4 1/2 decks instead of just 4 decks?
- Should I raise my bet at a count of +3 or +4?
- Can I beat the game if I use a betting spread of 1-to-4 units, or do I need 1-to-8?
- What's the best betting strategy if I only have $1,000 and the minimum bet is $10?
- What's my win rate if I quit the table when the count goes negative?
- What's my win rate if the house uses eight decks instead of six?

You **don't need** to run computer simulations to get the answers, and you don't need a degree in probability and statistics. You simply need a set of charts where you can look up the answers—the math has already been worked out. **Accurate for all counting systems** and any size bankroll, each report is 64 pages, with 44 pages of charts. There are five separate reports for games being dealt with 1, 2, 4, 6, and 8 decks. With any betting spread, the charts show the fluctuations you can expect in an hour of play, ten hours, 100 hours and more, so you can estimate the **best approach** to any game based on your actual bankroll. Get just the Reports that cover the games you currently play in, or get them all (and save $$$) to **be prepared** for any blackjack game anywhere.

Beat the 1-Deck Game: $25   **Beat the 6-Deck Game:** $25
Beat the 2-Deck Game: $25   **Beat the 8-Deck Game:** $25
Beat the 4-Deck Game: $25   **All five reports:** $95 (You save $30.00!)

To order, send $95 for all 5 reports (or $25 per report)—plus postage and handling to:
Cardoza Publishing, P.O. Box 98115, Las Vegas, NV 89193

SERIOUS BLACKJACK TITLES
BOOKS YOU MUST HAVE

THE BLACKJACK SHUFFLE TRACKER'S COOKBOOK
by Arnold Snyder
$49.95

In this 110-page professional report, Arnold Snyder reveals techniques never-before disclosed on the advanced and dangerous form of card counting known as shuffle tracking. These powerful techniques, known only to a few professional players, are way below the casino radar and allows players to use their winning skills long before the casinos ever get wind that there is an advantage player taking their money.

Included are numerous practice and testing methods for learning shuffle tracking, methods for analyzing and comparing the profit potential of various shuffles, the cost of errors; and much, much more. The hard data is organized into simple charts, and carefully explained. Note: If you are not currently a card counter, this book is not the place to start as shuffle tracking is not easy. This is for serious players only.

THE CARD COUNTER'S GUIDE TO CASINO SURVEILLANCE
by D.V. Cellini
$99.99

Learning the subtleties of playing winning blackjack undetected is an extremely difficult skill. It's hard enough to fool the casino employees you can see—dealers, floormen, pit bosses, and casino managers—but then there's the "eye," the behind-the-scenes surveillance department, with its biometric-identifying software along with the surveillance agents themselves. But now, for the first time ever, a long-time surveillance agent with vast experience and knowledge has emerged from the deep and dark recesses and exposed the inner workings to the light of scrutiny.

This 135-page special report is packed with inside advice on solo and team-play tactics; how to fly below the radar screen; how to confuse the agents and software; successful camouflage and counter-offensive techniques; and even sure-fire ways to get busted. This is a mighty weapon in any card-counter's arsenal—and it's fascinating reading for anyone interested in how casinos really work.

CARDOZA SCHOOL OF BLACKJACK
- Home Instruction Course - $200 OFF! -

At last, after years of secrecy, the **previously unreleased** lesson plans, strategies and playing tactics formerly available only to members of the Cardoza School of Blackjack are now available to the general public - and at substantial savings. **Now**, you can **learn at home,** and at your own convenience. Like the full course given at the school, the home instruction course goes **step-by-ste**p over the winning concepts. We'll take you from layman to **pro**.

MASTER BLACKJACK - Learn what it takes to be a **master player**. Be a **powerhouse**, play with confidence, impunity, and **with the odds** on your side. Learn to be a **big winner** at blackjack.

MAXIMIZE WINNING SESSIONS - You'll **learn how** to take a good winning session and make a **blockbuster** out of it, but just as important, you'll learn to cut your losses. Learn exactly when to end a session. We cover everything from the psychological and emotional aspects of play to altered playing conditions (through the **eye of profitability**) to protection of big wins. The advice here could be worth **hundreds (or thousands) of dollars** in one session alone. Take our guidelines seriously.

ADVANCED STRATEGIES - You'll learn the latest in advanced winning strategies. Learn about the **ten-factor**, the **ace-factor**, the effects of rules variations, how to protect against dealer blackjacks, the winning strategies for single and multiple deck games and how each affects you; the **true count**, the multiple deck true count variations, and much, much more. And, of course, you'll receive the full Cardoza Base Count Strategy package.

$200 OFF - LIMITED OFFER - The Cardoza School of Blackjack home instruction course, retailed at $295 (or $895 if taken at the school) is available here for just $95.

DOUBLE BONUS! - **Rush** your order in **now**, for we're also including, **absolutely free**, the 1,000 and 1,500 word essays, "How to Disguise the Fact that You're an Expert", and "How Not to Get Barred". Among other **inside information** contained here, you'll learn about the psychology of the pit bosses, how they spot counters, how to project a losing image, role playing, and other skills to maximize your profit potential.

To order, send $95 (plus postage and handling) by check or money order to:

Cardoza Publishing, P.O. Box 98115, Las Vegas, NV 89193

255